Snorkel Kaua'i

Guide to the Beaches and Snorkeling of Hawai'i • Judy & Mel Malinowski

Snorkel Kauai
Guide to the Beaches and Snorkeling of Hawaii

Second Edition © 2005 by Judy and Mel Malinowski

Published by: Indigo Publications
e-mail: indigo@snorkelguides.com

SAN 298-9921
Publisher's symbol: Indigo CA

Printed in China by C & C Offset Printing Co., Inc.

All landscape photography ©Mel Malinowski.
All underwater photography ©Jay Torborg unless otherwise noted.

Award-winning photographer Jay Torborg has been photographing nature for almost 30 years. Jay started out focusing on landscape photography, but over the last several years, his photographic interests have shifted toward wildlife and underwater photography. More of Jay's photography can be seen and purchased on his web site www.torborgphoto.com

Jay uses Nikon D1X professional digital SLRs with a wide range of professional Nikon lenses for most of his photography. For underwater photography, he uses this same camera mounted in a Seacam housing with two Ikelite 200 strobes.

About the cover: turtles come to certain locations called *cleaning stations* to have algae and parasites eaten off of their shells by Hawai'ian cleaner wrasses, or in this case by yellow tangs. Photo by Jay Torborg.

Thanks to the many kind-spirited people of Hawai'i who bring the spirit of aloha to all they do. Special thanks to Dr. John Randall and John Hoover for their inspiration, wonderful reference books on the sea life of our islands, and helpful counsel. Thanks to Danny Akaka for advising and teaching us. Through him, we have come to better understand the beauty and value of Hawai'ian language and culture.

ISBN 0-9646680-7-6
Library of Congress Control Number: 2001012345

Contents

Orientation

4   Kaua'i Road Map
6   Why Snorkel Kaua'i?

Ready

8   Basics
9   Gear Selection
18   Into the Water
24   Caring for Your Gear
26   Hazards

Sites

36   Where are Those Fish?
38   Site Index Map
40   Sites at a Glance
42   Northwest
60   Princeville
82   Northeast
96   East
130   Līhu'e
140   Po'ipū
170   Southwest
178   West

Excursions

194   Water

Useful Information

198   Marine Life
212   Weather
216   Language
218   Often Heard Myths

Reference

220   Index
224   About the Authors

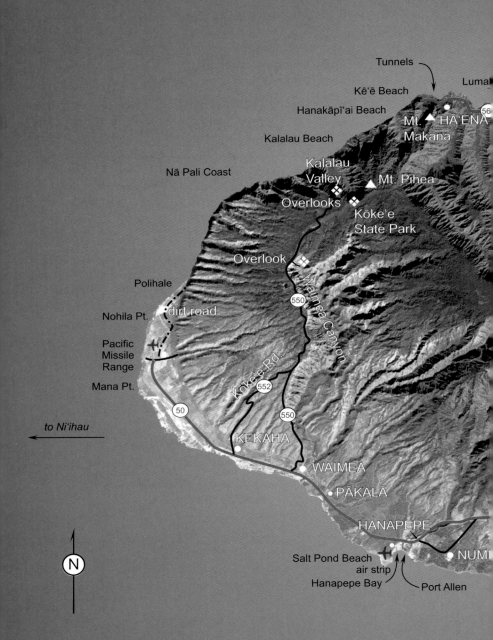

Tunnels

Kē'ē Beach

Luma

Hanakāpī'ai Beach

Mt. HĀ'ENA
Makana

Kalalau Beach

56

Nā Pali Coast

Kalalau
Valley

Overlooks

Mt. Pihea

Kōke'e
State Park

Overlook

Polihale

Waimea Canyon

550

Nohila Pt.

dirt road

Pacific
Missile
Range

Mana Pt.

Kōke'e Rd.

552

to Ni'ihau

550

50

KEKAHA

WAIMEA

PĀKALA

HANAPEPE

N

NUMI

Salt Pond Beach
air strip

Hanapepe Bay

Port Allen

Kaua'i Road Map

(Also see Snorkeling Site Index Map on page 38)

analei Bay

PRINCEVILLE

Kalihiwai Bay

Moku'ae'ae Island

Kīlauea Lighthouse

Kīlauea Bay

Larsen's Beach

Moloa'a Bay

HANALEI

KĪLAUEA

56

Kūhiō Hwy

Pāpa'a Bay

Anahola Bay

ANAHOLA

Pu'u 'Eu

KEALIA

Kumukumu Beach

KAPA'A

Mt. Wai'ale'ale 5148'

581

Kapa'a Beach

WAILUA

Mt. Kawaikini 5243'

Fern Grotto

56

Lydgate

570

Hanamā'ulu Bay

51

LĪHU'E

Līhu'e Airport

ĀWA'I

50

58

PUHI

Nāwiliwili Bay

KOLOA

Mt. Hā'upu

530

Kīpū Kai

PO'IPŪ

Māhā'ulepū Beaches

Keoneloa

Brennecke

bouting Horn

Po'ipū Beach

.ukui'ula

Hō'ai Bay

Kilometers

2   4   6

Miles

2   4   6

Why Snorkel Kaua'i?

Kaua'i, the Garden Isle, offers lush, spectacular scenery straight out
of your wildest tropical dreams. The oldest of the main Hawai'ian
islands, Kaua'i is dramatically mountainous and nearly surrounded
by fringing reef, with numerous pristine beaches. Most of the coast
can be reached by car, while the Nā Pali Coast, Ni'ihau and Lehua
Islands are just a boat excursion away.

Choose a snorkeling site by location, from gorgeous Kē'ē, at the
end of the road in the north, to secluded Māhā'ulepū in the south, or
child-safe Salt Pond in the west. Beginners will find Lydgate Park's
protected pond satisfying, while advanced snorkelers can roam the
extensive nearby reef when weather permits.

With few sites fully protected, everyone needs to learn how to
snorkel safely in Kaua'i. Seasons, swells, rain and tide level must all
be considered, so it's best to have plenty of choices of where to go on
a particular day. Few of Kaua'i's sites are well-marked, and some are
very difficult to find without detailed maps.

Snorkel Kaua'i makes it easy

An active vacation is memorable for adventure as well as relaxation.
Hassles and missteps finding out where to go can raise your blood
pressure and waste your time. We've done extensive research that
will help you quickly locate appropriate sites that fit your interests
and abilities, saving your valuable vacation hours.

Snorkeling sites in Hawai'i are sometimes tricky because of
changeable waves and currents, so it's best to get good advice before
heading out. Everyone has had their share of unpleasant experiences
due to vague directions as well as outdated or inaccurate information.
We have created the Snorkel Hawai'i series as that savvy snorkeling
buddy everyone needs. Many personal stories help bring the sea life
of Hawai'i more alive for our readers. See About the Authors on
page 224 if you want to know a little more about us.

We have snorkeled all the major sites listed, and many that are not
well known. The challenge lies in finding them quickly, as well as
how to enter and exit, and where to snorkel, so you'll have a safe and
rewarding experience. Our detailed maps, instructions and pictures
will ease the uncertainty, saving you time and effort.

Try to visit Kaua'i at least once in your life and by all means don't
miss the underwater world. Aloha!

—Judy and Mel Malinowski

Snorkeling is...

- easy
- relaxing
- fun
- floating on the surface of the sea
- breathing without effort through a tube
- peering into the water world through a mask
- open to any age, size, shape or ability

Who was the first snorkeler? As the fossil records include few petrified snorkels, we are free to speculate.

Among larger creatures, elephants are the pioneers and current champions, as they have known how to snorkel for countless generations. Once in a blue moon, you may see a elephant herd heading out to do lunch on an island off the coast of Tanzania, paddling along with their trunks held high. No one knows whether the hefty pachyderms enjoy the fish-watching, but you can bet a big liquid chuckle reverberates through the ranks of reef fish in the vicinity as the parade goes by.

As evolution continued, perhaps a clever member of the promising homo sapiens species saved his furry brow by hiding underwater from pursuers, breathing through a hollow reed. Masks came much later, so the fish probably looked a little fuzzy. Surviving to propagate his brainy kind, he founded a dynasty of snorkelers. Perhaps he actually liked the peaceful atmosphere down there, and a new sport was born.

Some of our readers may grumble that snorkeling is not a real sport: no rules, no score, no competition, scarcely aerobic, with hardly any equipment or clothing. We say to them: lighten up, you're on vacation!! Relax in the water—go for a long run later.

Incorrigible competitors can create their own competition by counting how many species they've seen or trying to spot the biggest or the most seen in one day. Everybody else can ease into the welcoming waters of Hawai'i and just have fun being a part of nature's colorful, salty, wet, ancient home.

Basics

To snorkel you need only two things:

Snorkel   Saves lifting your head once a minute, wasting energy and disturbing the fish.

Mask   While you can see (poorly) without one, it keeps the water out of your eyes and lets you see clearly.

Rent them inexpensively at many local shops or buy them if you prefer. It's all the back-to-basics folks need to snorkel in calm warm water, where there aren't any currents or hazards.

Savvy snorkelers often add a few items to the list, based on years of experience, such as:

Swimsuit   Required by law in many localities. Added benefit: saves you from an occasional all-body sunburn.

Fins   Good if you want to swim with ease and speed like a fish. Saves energy. A must in Hawai'i, due to occasional strong currents. They protect your tender feet too.

T-shirt   Simple way to avoid or minimize sunburn on your back. Available everywhere in many colors.

Sunscreen   To slather on the tender exposed backside skin of your legs, neck, and the backs of your arms. Not optional in Hawai'i for light-skinned snorkelers.

Lycra Skin   A great all-body cover-up for warm weather. Provides much better protection than a T-shirt, and saves gallons of sunscreen. Keeps you from leaving a sunscreen oil slick in your wake. Available in most dive shops, and a good investment.

Wetsuit   For some, the Hawai'ian waters seem a bit chilly, not exactly pool-warm. Wetsuits range from simple T-shirt-like tops to full suits. Worth considering. Fringe benefit: free sun protection!

You're almost ready to get wet. But wait! You want to know even more technical detail? Every sport has an equipment list—it's what keeps sporting goods stores in business and your garage shelves full.

8

Gear Selection

Good snorkeling gear enables you to pay attention to the fish instead of uncomfortable distractions. Poor equipment will make you suffer in little ways, from pressure headaches caused by a too-tight mask, to blisters on your feet from ill-fitting fins. Consider your alternatives carefully before buying and you'll have more fun later. This is a case of "pain, no gain." If it hurts, fix it, and you'll be glad you did.

Snorkel

Snorkels can be quite cheap. Be prepared to pony up $15 or more, however, if you want them to last awhile and be comfortable. You'll appreciate a comfortable mouthpiece if you plan to snorkel for long. Watch out for hard edges — a good mouthpiece is smooth and chewy-soft. Some of the more expensive mouthpieces swivel for comfort. We like that better than corrugated models.

Several new high-tech models have been designed to minimize water coming down the tube from chop or an occasional swell overtopping you. We looked at these with mild skepticism until a choppy snorkeling trip had us coughing and clearing our snorkels every third breath. With our new dry snorkels, that water never makes it to the mouthpiece.

Technology continues to advance, so you can now get a snorkel that will keep ALL of the water out, even if you dive beneath the surface. Don't ask us how they do it, but it works well! Even in very choppy conditions, you never worry about water coming in. We like the Ocean Master® dry snorkel, at about $40. It certainly makes learning to snorkel as easy as possible, although it's not a necessity.

These fancier snorkels do need care because you won't want a valve to fail just as you arrive at that perfect destination. In Hawai'i, repairs or replacements are available at most dive shops.

Snorkel Holder

This little guy holds your snorkel to your mask strap, so you don't keep dipping it in the sea. The standard is a simple figure 8 double loop that pulls over the snorkel tube, wraps around your mask strap, and then back over the tube. A hefty rubber band will work passably in a pinch. The downside of this type of snorkel holder is that it doesn't slide up and down easily, and often gets tangled with long

9

hair. The good news is that there is a better way available. The higher end snorkels often have a slot or movable ring that allows the snorkel to be adjusted easily. It slides easily rather than having to be tugged. The standard Scuba snorkel position is on your left side. You might as well get used to it there since you may dive eventually.

Mask

Nothing can color your snorkeling experience more than an ill-fitting mask (unless, of course, you get that all-body sunburn mentioned earlier). Don't settle for painful or leaky masks! If it hurts, it's not your problem — it's the mask that's wrong for you. Remember our snorkeling principle: "pain, no gain"!

Simple variety store masks can cost as little as $10. Top-quality masks from a dive shop run upwards of $60. Consider starting out with a rental mask, paying a bit extra for the better quality models. As you gain more experience, you'll be in a better position to evaluate a mask before you lock yourself into one style.

You need a good fit to your particular facial geometry. Shops often tell you to place the mask on your face (without the strap) and breathe in. If the mask will stay in place, then they say you have found a good fit. However, nearly all masks will stay on my face under this test, yet some leak later! You can do better.

Look for soft edges and a mask that conforms to your face even before drawing in your breath. There's a great deal of variance in where a mask rests on your face and how soft it feels, so compare very carefully. Look for soft and comfortable, unless you especially like having pressure headaches and don't mind looking like a very large octopus glommed on to your face.

Lack of 20-20 vision needn't cut into your viewing pleasure, but it does require a little more effort during equipment selection. Those who wear contact lenses can use them within their masks, taking on the risk that they'll swish out and float softly and invisibly down to the sea bed, perhaps to be found by a fossil hunter in the distant future, but certainly not by you. Use the disposable kind. Unless you use contacts, search for a correctable mask. Vision-correcting lens are available for many masks in 1/2 diopter increments.

If the mask you prefer doesn't offer standard correcting lenses, custom prescription lenses can be fitted to almost any mask. This

moorish idol

costs more and takes longer. Even bifocals are available. We happen to prefer the comfortable prescription masks made by SeaVision® which can be ordered with any custom correction. The cost is much like normal prescription lenses.

Mustaches create a mask leakage problem. As Mel likes the look of a mustache, he has coped with this his entire adult life. Some advise the use petroleum jelly or silicon compound to make a more effective seal. That doesn't appeal to him since he goes in and out of the water several times a day. It does help to choose a mask that rests high over the mouth and perhaps trim the top 1/8 inch or so off the center mustache, if it sticks up. Hair breaks the seal and allows water to seep into the mask slowly, so you'll still have to clear the mask occasionally. Mel has learned to tolerate half an inch of water in the bottom of his mask, though that doesn't work for everyone.

Someone who has struggled with a leaky mask may prefer having a purge valve. There are some clever higher-end purge valve masks. The challenge is how to fit in a purge valve without making it harder to pinch your nose when you equalize your ears during surface or scuba diving.

The conventional wisdom in Scuba is that purge valves are an unnecessary weak point. Nevertheless, there are experienced divers who use them. This isn't an issue snorkelers need worry about. If you find a purge valve mask that fits well, use it if you prefer.

11

Mask Strap

The strap that comes with the mask is OK, though it can tangle your hair. If you have your own mask and want it to slide on more easily, there's a comfortable strap available with adjustment by velcro. The back is made of wetsuit material — stretchy and soft. Cost is about $12 in dive shops. Since we get in and out so often, we happen to prefer this one to the regular strap, but it's a convenience for the frequent snorkeler rather than a necessity.

Fins

The simplest fins are basic (usually black) enclosed foot fins. These are one-piece molded rubber and slip right on to your bare feet. For warm water, basic snorkeling, these inexpensive fins are fine. We own several kinds of fins and still often choose the one-piece foot fins for lightness and compact packing. They seem to last forever and are inexpensive ($15-$25).

Why should anyone look further? Because it is possible to get better comfort and more thrust. Specialized fins are now made for higher performance. We tested three sets of fins, doing timed swims over a measured course. The basic fins discussed above went first. A set of fairly expensive, but rather soft, flexible strap-on fins cut the swim time by 20%, while ultra long, stiff-bladed enclosed-foot Cressi® fins cut it by 40%! These long surface diving fins are, however, a little long and awkward to use for most surface snorkeling.

Opinions vary about the merits of flexible fin blades versus stiff blades. We've tested both for snorkeling, and we prefer light, thin, stiff blades, hands down. We also prefer fins that don't float, which isn't an issue with Scuba divers, but can reduce a snorkeler's efficiency if they lift the fins too high in the water.

Our current favorites are Oceanic Vortex® fins, with a very comfortable molded shoe and split blades. They feel good on your bare feet, and seem to give you lots of speed for less effort.

You're better off with a medium blade foot fin for most snorkeling. Large diving fins are awkward for snorkeling, and require more leg strength than most non-athletes possess. The big diving fins do come in numerous shapes and colors, which some people are convinced will make them faster or perhaps more attractive. Speed is not the main aim of snorkeling, but has its uses. Faster fins do enable you to cover more territory and they also serve as excellent insurance in case you wander into a strong current. Unless it's absolutely certain that no current can carry you away, ALWAYS WEAR FINS!

As you look at more advanced fins, they split into two attachment methods with pros and cons to each type. We own both and pick the best for a particular situation.

ENCLOSED FOOT	Your bare foot slides into a stretchy, integral molded rubber shoe.
Advantages	The lightest, most streamlined and fish-like fit. It probably is the most efficient at transmitting your muscle power to the blade. We prefer this type when booties are not required for warmth or safety.
Disadvantages	The fins must be closely fitted to your particular foot size and shape. Some models may cause blisters. If you have to hike in to the entry site, you need separate shoes. This may preclude entering at one spot, and exiting elsewhere. If you hike over rough ground (a'a lava, for example) to get to your entry point, or the entry is over sharp coral or other hazards, these may not be the best choice.
STRAP-ON	Made for use with booties.
Advantages	Makes rough surface entry easy. Just hike to the entry point, head on into the water holding your fins in hand, lay back and pull on your fins. Exiting is just as easy. The bootie cushions your foot, making blisters unlikely. Widely used for Scuba.
Disadvantages	Less streamlined. The bootie makes your feet float up, so you may have trouble keeping your fins from breaking the surface.

No matter how good the fins, snorkeling for long hours may cause blisters — especially on the heel. No need to worry if you carry 3M Nexcare® waterproof bandages. These little essentials will do the job and stay in place well when wet. Buy them at a major pharmacy before your trip — they can be hard to find in the islands.

Reef Shoes or Booties

Walking with bare feet on a'a (sharp lava) or coral can shred your feet in a quick minute. There are fine reef shoes available that are happy in or out of the water. These are primarily for getting there, or wading around, as they don't really work that well with strap-on fins.

For the sake of the reef, don't actually walk on a reef with reef shoes, since each step kills hundreds of the little animals that make up the living reef.

Zip-on booties are widely used by divers and allow use of strap-on fins. They do float your feet — a disadvantage for snorkelers.

Keeping Time

One easy-to-forget item: a water-resistant watch. This needn't be expensive and is very useful for pacing yourself and keeping track of your sun exposure time.

"Water resistant" alone usually means that a little rain won't wreck the watch, but immersion in water may. When a designation like "to 10 meters" is added, it denotes added water-resistance; but the dynamic pressures from swimming increase the pressure, so choose 50 meters or greater rating to be safe even when snorkeling. Don't take a 50 meter watch Scuba diving, though — that requires 100-200 meter models.

Hawai'ian time is two hours earlier than Pacific Standard Time or three hours earlier than Pacific Daylight Time. Hawai'i doesn't observe Daylight Savings Time.

Body Suit

There are a variety of all-body suits that protect you from sun exposure and light abrasion, but provide no warmth. They are made from various synthetic fabrics — lycra and nylon being common. They cost much less than wetsuits and are light and easy to pack.

We usually bring ours along as a sun protection alternative in warmer conditions. If you don't want to look like a F.O.B. (Fresh Off the Boat) tourist, with a shocking pink outline of your swimsuit, plan ahead about sun protection. You'll sleep better if you do too. And the fish will not miss all that sunscreen fouling their water.

Wetsuit

In Kaua'i, water temperature on the surface varies from a low of about 72° F in March to a high of about 80° F in September. If you happen to be slender, no longer young or from a moderate climate, this can seem cold. Sheltered bays and tidepools can be a bit warmer while deeper water can be surprisingly cold. Fresh water runoff can also make water cooler than you might expect. We've snorkeled in March when we swore it was not a bit warmer than 65° off Kaua'i. Maybe not, but even two degrees cooler feels like six or eight!

Regardless of the exact temperature, the water is cooler than your body. With normal exertion, your body still cools bit by bit. After awhile, perhaps 30-45 minutes, you start feeling a little chilly. Later you begin shivering and eventually hypothermia begins.

We often snorkel for more than an hour. A thin, 3mm full wetsuit protects us from the sun while keeping us warm and comfortable. Off the rack suits are a bargain and fit most folks. Look for a snug fit at neck, wrists and ankles—if your suit is loose there, water will flow in and out, making you cold. If you have big feet and small ankles, get zippers on the legs if possible or you'll really have to struggle to remove the suit when it's wet.

Wetsuit wearers also get added range and buoyancy, and they hardly need a life jacket! Wearing a wetsuit, you can stay in the water without hypothermia for many hours—even in the winter. This could be comforting in the unlikely event that some strong current sweeps you off towards Fiji. There are few situations from which you can't rescue yourself if you're wearing a wetsuit and fins.

We've found a wetsuit favorite: Henderson Gold Core® wetsuits, made in Millville, New Jersey. The inside of this suit is coated with a gold-colored nylon that slides on easily wet or dry, and the inner surface dries very quickly. The three millimeter-thick version is light, warm enough for Hawai'i snorkeling and has extra stretch so it's comfortable and easy to get on and off. Thicker versions that are warmer are also available. Other types include Hyperstretch® (easier to get on and off) and Instadry®, which scarcely absorbs water.

Even Gold Core slides poorly on skin with dried-on sticky saltwater (as when you're getting in and out frequently on a multi-stop boat trip), though better than regular wetsuits. We found, however, that if you get wet first (in a beach shower, boat shower, or by jumping in), Gold Core slides on like teflon.

Dave Barry once described putting on a wetsuit as like wrestling with an octopus. Not this one! No more hanging onto the shower while your buddy tries to pull the wetsuit off your ankles with a winch. If you can afford the extra cost, the suit is superb. We had ours custom-made with longer arms and legs, and no rubberized kneepads. We like our wetsuits sleek and flexible, and never wear out the knees.

Swim Cap

If you have trouble with long hair tangling in your mask straps while snorkeling, get a lycra Speedo® swim cap. It may look silly, but it works, and also protects your scalp from too many rays.

Snorkeling Vest

It is possible to buy inflatable vests made for snorkeling. Some guidebooks and stores promote them as virtually essential. We've taken excursions that require all snorkelers to wear one. Other excursions encourage the use of flotation "noodles" or kick boards — whatever it takes to make you comfortable.

Vests are hardly necessary in salt water for most people, but can be useful if you can't swim a lick or won't be willing to try this sport without it. There is a possible safety edge for kids or older folks. If you do get a vest, you can give it to another beginner after you get used to snorkeling. You will discover that it takes little effort to float flat in the water while breathing through a snorkel.

If you feel you need extra flotation, consider using a light wetsuit instead. It simultaneously gives you buoyancy, sun and critter protection, and warmth.

Surface Diving Gear

For surface diving, bigger fins help your range. Those surreal-looking Cressi® fins that seem about three feet long will take you down so fast you'll be amazed. You'll also be amazed how few suitcases are big enough to accommodate them.

A long-fin alternative is to use a soft weight belt with from 2 to 4 pounds (more if you wear a wetsuit) — just enough to help you get under the surface without using up all your energy. As you descend, you become neutrally buoyant at about 15-20 feet so you don't have to fight popping up. Of course, the sword cuts two ways, since you must swim up under your own power in time to breathe.

Low Volume Masks

When you begin looking at masks, the variety can be bewildering. How can you figure out which design is best for you?

Inexpensive masks often have one large flat front glass. They're OK if the skirt of the mask fits you, although they're often a bit stiff and uncomfortable. They also tend to be far out from your face with a big air space. As you go up in price, the lenses tend to get smaller and closer to your eyes, as preferred by divers.

There is a good Scuba reason for this. These are called "low volume" masks. They contain less airspace and so require less effort to clear when water gets in. They also press less against your face when you go deeper and the pressure rises (if you forget to blow higher pressure air in through your nose) and hence are more comfortable when diving.

For a snorkeler this is of little importance, but it still should be considered as you select your mask. Many snorkelers go on to do some surface diving, as well as Snuba® or Scuba diving. When you dive down even 10 feet, the water pressure is considerable. At 32 feet, the air in your lungs and mask is compressed to half its volume. Unless you blow some air into your mask through your nose, the pressure on your face can be quite uncomfortable!

If your mask is flooded, which does happen, it is easier to clear out a low volume mask. So, while it's not the most important factor, if everything else is equal, low volume is better.

colonial cup coral

17

Into the Water

Getting Started

Now that you've assembled a nice collection of snorkel gear, you're ready to go! On a sunny tropical morning you're down at the water's edge. Little one-foot waves slap the sand lightly, while a soft warm breeze takes the edge off the intensity of the climbing sun. It's a great day to be alive and out in the water.

Going snorkeling, it's better to have no suntan lotion on your face or hands. You sure don't want it washing into your eyes to make them burn and water. Wear a nice big hat instead. You applied lotion to your back before you left, so it had time to become effective. Then you washed off your hands and rinsed them well so the lotion couldn't contaminate your mask later.

Or you could do like we do, and skip all the lotion. Being outside as much as we are, and in and out of the water, we prefer to carefully cover up instead—we find too much lotion hard on our skin. Big broad hats like your boat captain wears help. Comfortable cotton cover-ups look good and are cool. Lycra body suits or wetsuits in the water let you stay in for as long as you wish. Do watch out for reflected light on long boat trips, which can sneak in and sizzle your tender face.

convict tang

Checking Conditions

Take it nice and slow. Sit down and watch the waves for awhile. Check the slope of the beach. Consider whether there might be currents. Look for wave patterns, how big the biggest waves are and how far they wash up on the beach. When you see the pattern, you're ready to go. Set your gear down back well beyond the furthest watermarks on the sand. You don't want that seventh wave to sweep your gear away! Watch as long as it takes to be sure conditions aren't changing for the worse.

Gearing Up

Now defog the mask so that water vapor from your nose, or water leakage, won't bead up on your mask lens and spoil your view. There are several ways to defog that work well.

The classic solution is: SPIT. Spit on the inside of your dry mask lens, and rub it all around with your sunscreen-free finger. Step into the water, just out beyond the stirred up sand, and dip up a mask full of clear saltwater. Thoroughly rub and rinse off that spit, and dump the mask. Now you have prepared a mask that may be fog-resistant for the length of an average snorkel.

If you spit and polish, and still have fogging problems, there are several possible causes. Your mask may be gooped up with cosmetics, dried on saltwater residue or whatever other goo may be out there. A good cleaning with toothpaste may be in order (see Caring for Your Gear, page 24).

It's possible that you didn't actually wet all the surface with spit — perhaps because there were drops of water left on the lens. In that case, or if you just feel funny about spitting in your mask, you can use no-fog solution. It actually does work even better than spit. No-fog comes in small, handy, inexpensive bottles that seem to last forever because you use only a few drops at a time.

If you prefer to make your own, a mixture of half baby shampoo (so you don't irritate your eyes) and half water works fine. Some recipes add alcohol to the mix. Unless you are an excursion boat operator and use defog by the gallon, it's easier to just buy some!

Our favorite trick is to pre-apply no-fog solution to the dry masks as we load up our gear, and then let it dry. When you get to the water, just rinse out the mask thoroughly. This seems to last a long time.

Getting Comfortable

After you rinse your mask, try its fit. Adjust the mask strap and snorkel until they're comfortable. Hold the snorkel in your mouth without tightening your jaws. It can be quite loose without falling out. Putting your mask on long before you enter the water can cause it to fog from your exertions.

Getting Wet

Now retrieve your fins and walk back in the water, watching the waves carefully. NEVER turn your back on the ocean for long, lest a rogue wave sneak up on you and whack you good. The key is to stay alert and awake—especially on entry and exit.

If the bottom is sandy smooth, wade on out until you're about waist deep. Pull your mask on, making sure you remove any stray hair from under the skirt. Position the snorkel in your mouth and start breathing. You can practice this in a pool or hot tub.

Duck down in the water so you're floating and pull on your fins just like sneakers. Be sure no sand is trapped in the fins. Make a smooth roll to your stomach, pause to float and relax until you're comfortable, and you're off! Flip those fins and you have begun your re-entry into the sea.

As you float, practice steady breathing through the snorkel. Breathe slowly and deeply. People sometimes tense up at first and take short breaths. When this happens, you're only getting stale air from the snorkel rather than lots of fresh air from outside. If you ever feel tired or out of breath, don't take off your mask. Just stop as long as necessary, float, breathe easy and relax.

After you've become quite comfortable breathing this way, check how your mask is doing. Make sure it isn't leaking. Adjust the strap if needed. And keep adjusting until it's just right. Slide your snorkel strap to a comfortable position, with the tube pointing about straight up as you float looking down at about a 30° angle.

Swimming while snorkeling is easy once you've relaxed. No arms are required. What works best is to hold your arms straight back along your sides, keep your legs fairly straight and kick those fins slowly without bending your knees much. Any swimming technique will work, of course, but some are more tiring. Practice using the least amount of energy. Once you learn how to snorkel the easy way,

Motion Sickness

Motion sickness (such as seasickness, carsickness or airsickness) is a minor inner ear disorder which can really cut into your pleasure on the water, on long, curvy road trips or in choppy air. Fortunately, motion sickness is quite controllable these days. All it takes is a little advance planning to turn a potentially miserable experience into a normal, fun one. Don't let old fears keep you from great water adventures anymore.

Mel can get seasick just by vividly imagining a rocking boat, so he has personally tried just about every remedy. These field trials are a messy business, so we'll spare you the details, and just pass on what really works in our experience.

Forget the wrist pressure-point bands — they don't do the job for anyone we've ever met. You might as well put them in the closet along with your ultrasonic pest repeller, in our opinion.

The most effective remedy we've found so far is Meclizine®, a pill formerly available by prescription, but now over-the-counter. It works perfectly for Mel with no noticeable side effects. Alcohol can apparently interact with it to make you drowsy, though Mel has had a beer on excursions without falling asleep.

We learned about Meclizine when Jon Carroll, a columnist in the San Francisco Chronicle, reported that it had sufficed for him in 15-25' swells on the way to Antarctica. If it does the job there, it should handle all but the most radical of snorkeling excursions. It's always worked for us.

An over-the-counter alternative is Benadryl® usually used as a decongestant. It can also be effective against motion sickness. Ginger is also claimed to be effective. As much as we enjoy ginger as a spice, we cannot substantiate that it helps at all.

Use these medicines carefully and only after consulting your doctor. In some cases, you must avoid alcohol, other drugs or diving, since these medications can produce drowsiness.

you can use all the power you like touring large areas as if you were a migrating whale. But if you're breaking the surface with your fins, going "splash, plunk, splash", you're wasting energy. Be cool and smooth and quiet like a fish, and you'll swim like a dolphin.

eyestripe surgeonfish

Clearing Your Mask

Eventually you will need to practice clearing your mask. The Scuba method: take a deep breath, then tip your head up, but with the mask still under the surface. Press your palm to the top of the mask against your forehead, or hold your fingers on the top of the mask and exhale through your nose. This forces water out the bottom of the mask.

Taking It Easy

Relax and try not to push yourself too hard. Experienced snorkelers may urge you on faster than you're comfortable because they've forgotten how it feels to get started. As your experience builds, you'll find it easy too. It's like learning to drive a car. Remember how even a parking lot seemed like a challenge? It helps to practice your beginning snorkeling in a calm easy place—with a patient teacher. With a little persistence, you'll soon overcome your fears and be ready. Don't feel like you should rush. Play around and have fun!

Pacing

When you're having a good time, it's easy to forget and over extend yourself. That next rocky point beckons, and then a pretty spot beyond that. Pretty soon, you're many miles from home and getting tired. Getting cold and overly tired can contribute to poor judgement in critical situations, making you more vulnerable to injury. Why risk turning your great snorkeling experience into a disaster? Learn your limits, and how to pace yourself.

Our favorite technique: If we plan on a one-hour snorkel, we watch the time and start heading back when we've been in the water 30 minutes. If the currents could run against us on the way back, we allow extra time/energy. We like to start by swimming against the current, making the trip home easy and quick.

If you're cruising along, making great time, pay extra attention. Rather than being a snorkeling superman all of a sudden, you may be drifting along with a fast current. Stop and check the drift by watching the coral below you, and plankton in the water. If there is a current, allow extra time/energy for swimming back against it. Or if you're towing your reef shoes along, sometimes you can enjoy the ride and walk back (assuming you're sure there's a good exit ahead). You can use your fins for shade.

Knowing Your Limits

Have you heard the old saloon saying: "Don't let your mouth write checks that your body can't cover"?

Let's paraphrase this as "Don't let your ego take you places your body can't get you back from." Consider carefully how well-conditioned your legs are, so you'll have enough reserve to be able to make it back home, and then some in case of an emergency.

Snorkeling Alone

In your enthusiasm for the reef, you may wind up in this situation: your significant other prefers watching sports on ESPN to snorkeling one afternoon, and you're sorely tempted to just head out there alone. Don't do it. Snorkeling, done in buddy teams, is a pretty safe recreation, especially if conditions are favorable. Just as in Scuba diving, having a buddy along reduces the risk of a small problem becoming a big problem or even a fatal problem. We won't spell out all the bad things that could happen; we trust your imagination.

Caring for Your Gear

You just had a great snorkeling experience — now you can thank the gear that helped make it possible, by taking good care of it.

Rinse and Dry

If there are beach showers, head right up and rinse off. Salt residue is sticky and corrosive. Rinse salt and sand off your wetsuit, fins, mask and snorkel before the saltwater dries. If you can, dry your gear in the shade. It's amazing how much damage sun can do to the more delicate equipment — especially the mask. When the sun odometer hits 100,000 miles, you can kiss those soft parts good-bye.

Safety Inspections

Keep an eye on vulnerable parts after a few years (strap, snorkel-holder, buckles). Parts are usually easy to find in Hawai'i, but not in the middle of a snorkeling trip unless you're on a well-equipped excursion.

If you use any equipment with purge valves, keep an eye on the delicate little flap valves, and replace them when they deteriorate. Masks and snorkels are useless when the valves give way. Remember that many snorkels now have a purge valve at the bottom.

Clean Your Mask

A mask needs a thorough cleaning between trips. Unless your mask instructions advise otherwise, use a regular, non-gel toothpaste to clean the lens inside and out, polishing off accumulated goo. Wash the toothpaste off with warm water, using your finger to clean it well.

peacock grouper

Sign Language

Any serious snorkeler should bother to learn some basic signs starting with some of the standard Scuba ones such as *OK* — meaning "Are you OK?", which should be answered with another *OK*; *palm up* for "stop", *wobbling hand* for "problem", and *thumb down*, meaning "heading down" (in this case referring to surface diving). This is an essential safety issue making it possible to communicate even if slightly separated or underwater. See a few of the signs below.

It's also a nuisance to take the snorkel out of your mouth every time you want to say "Did you see that moray!?!" Worse yet is trying to understand your buddy who frantically gestures and mumbles through the snorkel while you play charades. With a frequent snorkeling companion it's fun to develop signs for the creatures you might see. Eel can be indicated by three fingers looking like an E or by a wavy line drawn in the water. Then all you have to do is point and there it is!

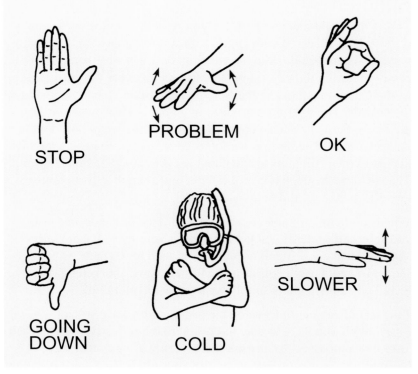

STOP

PROBLEM

OK

GOING DOWN

COLD

SLOWER

Hazards

Life just isn't safe. Snorkeling has a few hazards that you should know and avoid if possible. You already know the dangers of car and air travel, yet you mustered your courage and decided that a trip to Hawai'i was worth the risks. You took reasonable precautions like buckling your seat belt. Well, if you're sensible about it, you're probably safer in the water than while driving to get to the water.

Some people are hesitant to snorkel because they imagine meeting a scary creature in the water. But wouldn't you rather be able to see what's down there when you're swimming? We much prefer to see whatever you might step on, run into or encounter. The realities are seldom scary, and often beautiful instead. Don't let exaggerated risks keep you from enjoying life to the fullest.

We don't think it makes sense to overemphasize certain lurid but unlikely dangers (such as sharks) and pay no attention to the more likely hazard of sunburn which causes more aggravation to tourists.

Sunburn

This is the worst medical problem you're likely to face — especially if you weren't blessed with genetically sun-resistant skin. Use extra water-resistant sunblock in the water and always wear some kind of cover-up during the day. Some people need to avoid the sun entirely from 10 a.m. to 3 p.m., so that's a good excuse to go early and avoid the crowds. The top (or open) deck of a boat is a serious hazard to the easily-burned because bounced rays from the water will double your exposure. The best protection is covering up. Evidence mounts that sunscreen still allows skin damage even though it stops burning. Thanks to ozone depletion, we can get more sun in a given hour these days than we did many years ago.

When snorkeling, omit sunscreen on your face or hands, because you'll be sorry later if you get the stuff in your eyes. It can really sting and make it difficult to see well enough to navigate back to shore. To avoid using gallons of sunblock, some snorkelers wear lycra body suits. Others simply wear some old clothing.

Take an old sun hat to leave on the beach with your gear bag, especially if you have to hike midday across a reflective white beach. Take old sunglasses that are not theft-worthy. If you must leave prescription glasses on the beach, use your old ones. Kaua'i is a great

Understanding Waves

Waves are travelling ripples in the water, mostly generated by wind blowing over large expanses of water. Having considerable energy, the waves keep going until something stops them. They may travel many thousands of miles before dissipating that energy. Here is the wellspring of the breaking surf. That beautiful surf can also be the biggest danger facing snorkelers.

Take time to sit on a high point and watch the waves approaching the coast, and you will see patterns emerge. Usually there is an underlying groundswell from one direction, waves that may have originated in distant storms. This is the main source of the rhythmical breaking waves, rising and falling in size in noticeable patterns. Sometimes there will be a smaller secondary groundswell from another direction. Often, there will be a series of small waves, followed by one or more larger waves, and the cycle repeats. Pay attention to the patterns and it will be less likely that you'll get caught by surprise.

Local winds add extra energy in their own directions. In Hawai'i, snorkeling is usually easiest in the mornings, before the daily winds create chop and larger waves. Most excursions head out early to make sure they have smooth sailing and calm snorkeling. Sometimes afternoon excursions are offered at reduced prices to compensate for expected rougher conditions.

Occasionally a set of larger waves or a single large rogue wave comes in with little or no warning. A spot that was protected by an offshore reef suddenly has breaking waves. This change can happen while you're out, and make coming back difficult.

Our single worst moment in many years of snorkeling and diving was at Po'ipū Beach Park in Kaua'i after Hurricane 'Iniki had scattered boulders under the water. We had no problem snorkeling around the boulders in a light swell, protected by the reef further out. Suddenly much larger waves crossed the reef and began breaking over us, sweeping everyone back and forth among and against the boulders. Ouch!

Since then we have been extra careful to avoid potentially hazardous situations. We always take time to study the waves before entering and ponder what would happen if they suddenly grew much larger, and what our strategy would be. Sometimes we just head for a calmer beach.

place to find amazingly cheap sunglasses and flip-flops. For long hours in the sun, look into the better sunglasses that carefully filter all the most damaging rays.

Rip Currents

Hawai'i does not have large barrier reefs to intercept incoming waves. Few of Kaua'i's beaches are well-protected from powerful ocean swell—which is especially apparent in the winter or during storms.

Waves breaking against a shore push volumes of water up close to the shore. As this piles up, it has to flow back to the ocean, and often flows sideways along the shore until it reaches a convenient, often deeper-bottomed exit point. There, a fast, narrow river of water flows out at high speed. Rip currents, which can carry swimmers out quickly, are of limited duration by their very nature and usually stop no more than 100 yards out.

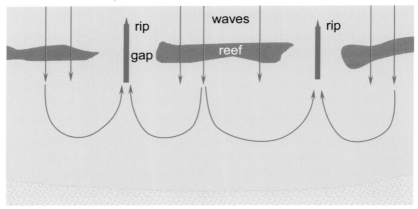

Sometimes it's possible to swim sideways, but often it's better to simply ride it out. Don't panic. Although the current might be very strong, it won't take you far or drown you, unless you exhaust yourself by swimming against it. It's very easy to float in salt water until help arrives—assuming you're at a beach where someone can see you. Don't try to swim in through waves where there's any chance of being mashed on lava rocks or coral. Don't swim against the current to the point of exhaustion. When in doubt, float and conserve your energy, while you plan the safest way out.

Even at the most protected beaches all the water coming in must get out, so when swells are up, there's a current somewhere. Big waves beyond the breakwater may seem harmless, but the more water comes in, the more must get out. This is a good reason to ALWAYS wear fins even when the inner reef is calm.

Rip currents should not be confused with offshore currents, such as the infamous "Tahiti Express". There are some major flows of water offshore that can be faster than you can swim, even with fins. Do be alert and careful if you swim out beyond rocky points. Or send us a postcard from Tahiti.

Hypothermia

Open ocean water is always cooler than your body, and it cools you off more rapidly than the air. With normal exertion, your body still cools bit by bit. After awhile (perhaps 30-45 minutes) most of us start feeling chilly. Later, shivering begins. When your temperature drops even further, hypothermia sets in. When your body temperature has dropped enough, your abilities to move and even think become surprisingly impaired. It can sneak up on you.

We used to think hypothermia was just an interesting concept, until it happened to us after a long snorkel in some unusually cold water. We were shivering, but having a great time, and snorkeled on and on. Fortunately, we noticed the decrease in our co-ordination and headed in while we still could. You'd have laughed to see us stumbling clumsily out of the waves. We headed straight for the nearest jacuzzi (not recommended for full-blown hypothermia!). As we warmed up, our limbs tingled like fizzy water was going through our veins.

One of the first symptoms of hypothermia is poor judgement. Buddies can watch out for each other better than you can watch out for yourself alone — one example of the benefits of having a partner. Check up on each other often in cold conditions.

As soon as you are aware that you're cold, it's time to plan your way back. When shivering starts, you should head for shore. Be particularly careful in situations requiring all your judgement and skill to be safe, especially when diving, night snorkeling, dealing with waves, or when anticipating a difficult exit from the water.

In Kaua'i, it's usually easy to warm up rapidly since the air temperature is fairly warm at sea level. Even without hypothermia, it's good to warm up between snorkels. If you came by car, it will probably be nicely solar-heated by the time you return.

Sea Urchins

Probably the most common critter injury is stepping on a spiny sea urchin and walking away with lots of spines under your skin. The purple-black spiny sea urchins with long spines tend to appear in groups and favor shallow water, so watch carefully if you see even one — it probably has friends. Full-foot flippers or booties help a lot, but don't guarantee protection. Watch where you put your hands — especially in shallow water.

Many folks recommend seeing a doctor for urchin spine slivers. Others prefer to just let the spines fester and pop out weeks later. Remove as much spine as you can. Vinegar (or other acidic liquid) will make it feel better. Soaking in Epsom salts helps and the small spines will dissolve in a few weeks, but definitely see a doctor at any sign of infection. Don't wait for blood poisoning to set in!

banded sea urchin

Barracudas

The great barracuda can grow to two meters, has sharp teeth and strong jaws, and swims like a torpedo. For years Judy has removed earrings before swimming after hearing rumors that they attract barracuda, but we've uncovered absolutely no confirming reports of severed earlobes attributable to jewelry. But they can bite!

Barracudas are capable of seriously injuring a swimmer so should be taken seriously. Those teeth are just as sharp as they look. Barracudas appear to have attitude, and apparently sometimes do. Our own preference is to respect their territory and allow them some space. Other varieties of barracuda such as the smaller Heller's barracuda appear more innocuous. Appearances can deceive, however.

Once a four-foot great barracuda swam directly beneath us in the Caribbean and appeared annoyed that we were invading his home territory (or so we thought from the fierce look on

great barracuda

his face). A usually calm and steady German surgeon headed up the nearest rocks as if she could fly. The rest of us snorkeled by him repeatedly with no problem, but didn't appreciate the look he gave us. We later came to realize that they always look grumpy, but seldom literally bite us, like some folks you may know. Perhaps the bigger danger comes from eating the delicious barracuda meat, sometimes containing ciguatera, which is a potent neurotoxin.

Sea Jellies

The Portuguese man-of-war floats on top, looking like a sail fin one to four inches in size, with long stinging filaments that are quite painful. Stay out of the water if you see one. Even avoid dead ones on the sand! They're very pretty in lovely shades of purple, but can cause severe pain.

sea jelly

Vinegar or unseasoned meat tenderizer helps ease the sting and helps stop the release of venom from the stinging cells if tentacles are clinging to you. Use wet sand as a last resort. If you feel ill, see a doctor right away. If sea jellies are present, locals will know which ones are harmful. Sea jellies have seldom been a problem for us in Hawai'i. In all our years in the water, we've only been stung by a Portuguese man-of-war once, not in Hawai'i, and it wasn't serious.

31

A reader recently reported getting little nips that were annoying. These could have been little bits of hydroids floating around, or possibly small stinging sea jellies. Wearing a wetsuit or lycra would have taken care of that. Generally, these little nips have no long lasting effects, so it's best to not panic. Do avoid rubbing bare skin against mooring ropes, which often are covered with hydroids.

Rays

Sting rays prefer to avoid you, but hang out on the bottom where they're easy to step on. They prefer resting in calm water that is slightly warmer than the surrounding area—just the areas favored by people for swimming. Step on them and they may sting you, so the injury is usually to the foot or ankle. They can inflict a serious or painful sting to people—especially children. It's best to get immediate first aid and follow up with medical assistance.

In this case snorkelers have an advantage over swimmers because snorkelers can see sting rays and easily avoid them. In Maui we've seen them swim between children's legs in shallow water at Kapalua

cleaner wrasse on spotted eagle ray

Bay and were amazed to see how adept the rays were at avoiding people. They really try to steer clear.

Manta rays don't sting, but they're much larger. They are often six to eight feet across, weighing several hundred pounds. They maneuver beautifully, and so they don't pose any danger. With a little luck and some planning, you may see one of these beautiful creatures.

Poisonous Fish

Lionfish (also called turkeyfish) and scorpionfish have spines which are very poisonous. Don't step on or touch them! Their poison can cause serious pain and infection or allergic reaction, so definitely see a doctor if you have a close, personal encounter with one. Fins or booties can help protect your tender feet.

Mel Malinowski

Hawai'ian turkeyfish

Scorpionfish can blend in so well along the bottom in shallow water that they're easy to miss. Turkeyfish, though, are colorful and easy to spot. Since these fish are not abundant in Hawai'i, they are treasured sightings for snorkelers. You are not likely to see one while shallow-water snorkeling.

Eels

Eels are rarely aggressive and often tamed by divers. Most do possess a formidable array of teeth, which should be avoided. An eel bite can definitely cause serious bleeding requiring prompt medical attention. Another reason not to snorkel alone!

whitemouth moray eel

33

Eels are fascinating and easy to find in Hawai'i. Count on eels to make every effort to avoid you, so there's no need to panic at the sight of one—even if it's swimming freely. Eels aren't interested in humans as food, but they do want to protect themselves and can usually do so with ease by slipping away into the nearest hole. Do we need to warn you to keep your hands out of crevices in the coral?

Cone Shells

The snails inside these pretty black and brown-decorated shells can fire a poisonous dart. The venom can cause a serious reaction or even death—especially to allergic persons. If in doubt, head for a doctor. If you never pick up underwater shells, you should be OK.

Drowning

Not likely to happen to you, but we want to help you become so alert and prepared that you have a safe vacation. Accidental drowning is a very preventable tragedy.

We looked up the statistics for the past 30 years, and they are both comforting and cautionary. Only an average of 6-7 folks drown each year in Kaua'i. A much lower number than fatalities from auto wrecks, industrial accidents, or probably even accidents around the home, but not a group you want to join.

A couple things stand out about who are the victims. Three out of four victims are visitors. Not too surprising, since you assume locals are more aware of the hazards. But nine out of ten are males, mostly 20 to 50 years old! You'd think this would be a low-risk group with enough sense to take care of themselves.

What leads these fellows to get into a dangerous situation? Well, some guys just can't help overrating their athletic prowess, and perhaps underestimate the power of the ocean.

Some locations seem distinctly more hazardous. Hanakāpī'ai Beach, first stop in on the Kalalau trail, is the leader. Make the tiring, hot hike, and then the water looks so refreshing! Then the riptide sweeps you out without fins, you swim to exhaustion, and the rest is history.

Wailua/Lydgate is second. It's very unlikely the victims were swimming in the protected pond in Lydgate Park that we recommend. It's the surf-pounded beach areas that are the real hazard here. Lumaha'i is third, with Polihale, Po'ipū, and Kapa'a trailing.

It's easy to swim and snorkel in Kaua'i safely. Improve your odds by picking protected beaches when the surf is pounding. Don't overestimate your stamina, or swim alone. Perhaps you might also follow our personal rule: always wear fins when swimming in the open ocean in Hawai'i—no matter how calm the water seems!

Sharks

Sharks are seldom a problem for snorkelers—people are not on their menu unless mistaken for legitimate prey or really obnoxious tourists. In Hawai'i many of the modest number of verified shark attacks have occurred off O'ahu, with tiger sharks the major perpetrator, and surfers the most common target because they look like seals. Sharks hunt in murky river runoff, but most snorkelers avoid these conditions anyway (our recommendation, too).

Mel Malinowski

blacktip reef shark

Statisticians tell us that you're more likely to be killed by a pig than a shark. We take great comfort in that, as I'm sure you do, too; though we've quit eating bacon just in case.

Some people will suggest you can pet, feed or even tease certain types of shark. We personally would give sharks a bit of respect and leave them entirely in peace. Most sharks are well-fed on fish and not all that interested in ordinary tourists, but it's hard to tell by looking at a shark whether it has had a bad day.

Sharks especially feed late in the day or at night, causing some people to prefer to enjoy the water more in the morning or midday. If you're in an area frequented by sharks, this might be good to keep in mind. We must admit that we snorkel at any hour, and occasionally night snorkel. The few sharks we have seen have all been midday.

In Kaua'i, with luck, you might possibly see sandbar, black-tip, white-tip or even hammerhead sharks—more often in deep water sites like Ahukini Landing or Hanalei Bay. Of these, only hammerhead sharks should be avoided. Unless you're a surfer, your chances of ever encountering a tiger shark are very slim.

35

Snorkeling Sites

Where are those big beautiful fish?

Kaua'i, with an abundance of sandy beaches, has many long stretches of fringing reef which provide snorkeling on all sides of the island. With this much reef, the snorkeling is often better than the swimming. The reef here is more developed than at any of the other main Hawai'ian islands because Kaua'i has been around the longest.

The Garden Isle is considerable less developed than the other islands, and has a smaller population. No other island has quite the lush tropical beauty of Kaua'i. It's lush for a reason—ample rainfall! Come prepared for the weather to be unpredictable with chances of very heavy rain and wind. Often you can snorkel with no problem in spite of the weather by driving to another beach that is drier or less choppy. Most of the coast is within easy driving distance, except for the Nā Pali Coast, where you won't find any roads at all.

The site section begins at the end of the highway in the far northwest, where the Nā Pali Coast begins. Kē'ē Beach and Tunnels are two excellent and scenic spots along this green and lush far corner of Kaua'i. Here, rivers from the nearly high mountains emerge at sandy beaches with broad reefs offshore. Winter brings huge waves from the north to this part of the island, making the beaches off-limits for nearly any sport except surfing. Rain showers are intense, but may last only a short time. Longer storms bring murky run-off to the bays. But the sun always comes back, and when conditions are favorable, these gorgeous northwest beaches are glorious.

Princeville offers small secluded beaches about 200 feet below the bluff, and plenty of luxurious condominiums nearby. The hikes to get to them are pretty and pleasant, and well worth the effort.

Northern Kaua'i has many long sandy beaches. A few, such as two-mile long 'Anini and the Tunnels area are well-protected by a large fringing reef. Others, like Kauapea, offer no protection from swells and surf. Still, when surf is low, snorkeling is good at these beaches.

The eastern side of Kaua'i is exposed to the heavy east swell nearly all year. While these beaches often have broad, low reefs, the relentless swells from the east make them difficult and dangerous during much of the year. Two or three weeks a year, they flatten, and are calm and easy to snorkel. If you are lucky enough to be there when that happens, jump in! At all other times, be cautious.

There are some exceptions. Lydgate Park (completely protected by a man-made breakwater) and Kalapakī (inside of Nāwiliwili Bay) are almost always safe. Anahola Beach Park offers some protection from swells at Anahola Bay's south end.

The southeast contains some of Kaua'i's least developed spots in the Māhā'ulepū area near Po'ipū, where sand dunes and isolation are both appealing and easy to reach. This area is quite windswept, and often is better-suited for flying kites than picnicing.

The popular Po'ipū area in the south provides plenty of snorkeling beaches, the widest assortment of accommodations, and more hours of sun and less rainfall. Po'ipū has quite a variety of snorkeling sites within easy driving distance, from small to large, calm to challenging. Choose the broad sandy beach shared by the Sheraton Hotel and the Kiahuna Plantation, or try less scenic Kōloa Landing or Hō'ai Bay. The south is a good bet in winter, when the north is likely to be much rougher and wetter.

As the highway continues clockwise, it reaches the big western beaches. Barking Sands beaches stretch for miles. Most of the Hawai'ian islands have the best snorkeling on the protected leeward southwest and west sides. Kaua'i's western beaches, however, tend to be very rough, due to their exposure to the vast Pacific Ocean. When swells roll in from the northeast, they wrap around and affect western Kaua'i. Prevailing swell and currents travel around Kaua'i and converge off Barking Sands, making some impressive large roller coaster swells. Snorkeling and swimming is usually dangerous along this coast. Salt Pond Beach Park is an exception inside its natural breakwater.

Five miles past the far western end of the paved highway lies secluded Polihale Beach, on the southern flank of the rugged Nā Pali Coast. Several small reef-fringed beaches can provide good snorkeling off this dramatic coast, when the weather cooperates. All must be accessed by excursion or kayak, unless you plan as much as a year ahead to secure a hiking permit, and then make the long, strenuous hike from the northern trail head near Kē'ē beach.

Excursions from Hanalei and Port Allen both offer trips to the Nā Pali Coast as well as Ni'ihau Island and Lehua Island, a pristine volcanic crater about a mile north of Ni'ihau.

Because swell direction and exact angle of each beach is so important in Kaua'i, we've made sure to draw each map with north at the top. We've also listed them in clockwise direction.

Snorkel Site Index Map

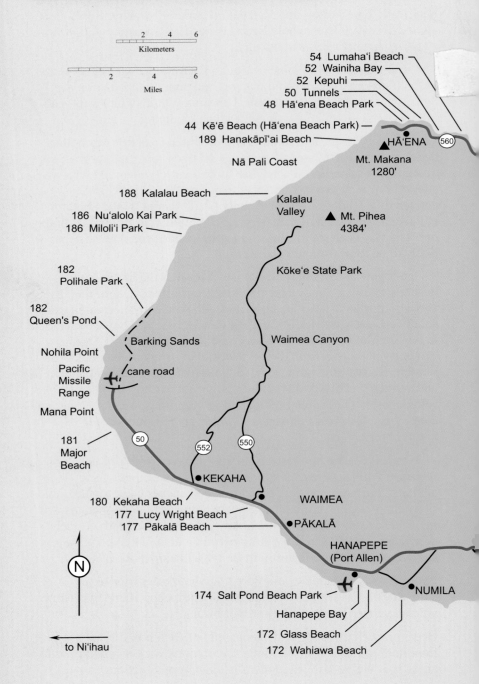

2   4   6
Kilometers

2   4   6
Miles

54 Lumaha'i Beach
52 Wainiha Bay
52 Kepuhi
50 Tunnels
48 Hā'ena Beach Park
44 Kē'ē Beach (Hā'ena Beach Park)
189 Hanakāpī'ai Beach

HĀ'ENA
560

Mt. Makana
1280'

Nā Pali Coast

188 Kalalau Beach

Kalalau
Valley

▲ Mt. Pihea
4384'

186 Nu'alolo Kai Park
186 Miloli'i Park

Kōke'e State Park

182
Polihale Park

182
Queen's Pond

Barking Sands

Waimea Canyon

Nohila Point

Pacific
Missile
Range

cane road

Mana Point

181
Major
Beach

50

552

550

KEKAHA

180 Kekaha Beach

WAIMEA

177 Lucy Wright Beach
177 Pākalā Beach

PĀKALĀ

HANAPEPE
(Port Allen)

N

NUMILA

174 Salt Pond Beach Park

Hanapepe Bay

172 Glass Beach
172 Wahiawa Beach

to Ni'ihau

38

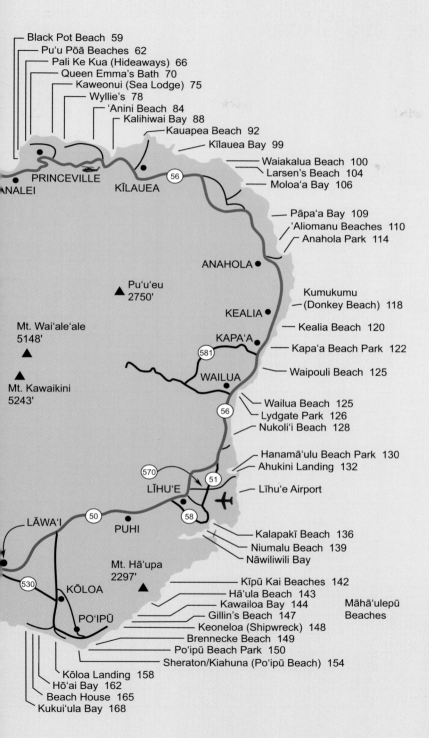

Black Pot Beach 59
Pu'u Pōā Beaches 62
Pali Ke Kua (Hideaways) 66
Queen Emma's Bath 70
Kaweonui (Sea Lodge) 75
Wyllie's 78
'Anini Beach 84
Kalihiwai Bay 88
Kauapea Beach 92
Kīlauea Bay 99
Waiakalua Beach 100
Larsen's Beach 104
Moloa'a Bay 106

Pāpa'a Bay 109
'Aliomanu Beaches 110
Anahola Park 114

Kumukumu
(Donkey Beach) 118
Kealia Beach 120
Kapa'a Beach Park 122
Waipouli Beach 125

Wailua Beach 125
Lydgate Park 126
Nukoli'i Beach 128

Hanamā'ulu Beach Park 130
Ahukini Landing 132
Līhu'e Airport

Kalapakī Beach 136
Niumalu Beach 139
Nāwiliwili Bay

Kīpū Kai Beaches 142
Hā'ula Beach 143
Kawailoa Bay 144   Māhā'ulepū
Gillin's Beach 147   Beaches
Keoneloa (Shipwreck) 148
Brennecke Beach 149
Po'ipū Beach Park 150
Sheraton/Kiahuna (Po'ipū Beach) 154
Kōloa Landing 158
Hō'ai Bay 162
Beach House 165
Kukui'ula Bay 168

PRINCEVILLE
ANALEI
KĪLAUEA
56

ANAHOLA

Pu'u'eu
2750'

Mt. Wai'ale'ale
5148'

KEALIA

KAPA'A
581
WAILUA

Mt. Kawaikini
5243'

56

570
51
LĪHU'E

LĀWA'I   50
PUHI
58

530   KŌLOA

Mt. Hā'upa
2297'

PO'IPŪ

39

Sites at a Glance

	Snorkeling	Entry	Sandy beach	Restroom	Showers	Picnic area	Scenic	Shade
Kē'ē Beach	A	1	•	•	•	•	•	
Tunnels	A	1	•	•	•	•	•	•
Kepuhi Beach	A	1-3	•			•	•	
Lumaha'i Beach	C	1-2	•			•	•	
Hanalei Bay beaches	C	1	•	•	•	•	•	
Pu'u Pōā (Princeville)	B	1	•	•	•	•	•	
Pali Ke Kua (Hideaways)	B	2	•			•	•	
Queen Emma's Bath	A	1				•		
Kaweonui (Sea Lodge)	A	1-2	•			•	•	
'Anini Beach	C	1	•	•	•	•	•	
Kalihiwai Bay	C	1-2	•			•	•	
Kauapea (Secret Beach)	C	3	•			•	•	
Kīlauea Bay	C	3	•			•	•	
Larsen's Beach	C	3	•		•	•	•	
Moloa'a Bay	B	1-2	•			•	•	
Anahola Bay	B	1-2	•	•	•	•	•	•
Kumukumu (Donkey Beach)	B	3	•			•		
Kapa'a Beach	B	1-2	•	•	•	•	•	
Lydgate Beach Park	A	1	•	•	•	•	•	
Ahukini Landing	A	1-2						
Kalapakī Beach	C	1-2	•	•	•	•	•	
Māhā'ulepū beaches	B	1-3	•			•	•	
Po'ipū State Park	B	1-2	•	•	•	•	•	
Sheraton/Kiahuna Beach	B	1-2	•	•	•	•	•	
Kōloa Landing	A	1-2						
Hō'ai Bay	B	1-2						
Beach House	A	1-2	•	•	•		•	
Salt Pond Beach	A	1	•	•	•	•	•	
Polihale Beach Park	C	3	•	•	•	•	•	
Lehua Island	A	1				•		

A	Excellent	1	Easy
B	Good	2	Moderate
C	Fair	3	Difficult

Page	Map page	
44	45	small cove, spectacular location, popular, don't miss
50	49	snorkel at Tunnels, facilities at Hā'ena, tops when calm
52	53	good in summer, large reef, access around homes
54	55	little coral, few fish, beautiful, sometimes dangerous
56	57	better for swimming, winter can bring huge waves
62	63	room to explore if calm, turtles, 171 steps down
66	67	very steep hike down cliff, shallow inner reef
70	71	enchanting small natural pool at base of cliffs
75	77	high tide necessary, worth hike down cliffs, secluded
84	85	high tide best, vast shallow inner reef to explore
88	89	pretty, somewhat protected bay with kayaking
92	93	beautiful long beach, variable conditions, pleasant hike
99	83	short hike, pretty bay with trees, but best for surfing
104	103	rarely calm, long fringing reef, too shallow inside
106	107	pretty & lush valley, walk to ends of beach to snorkel
114	115	high tide best, lovely spot, room to explore when calm
118	119	pretty, often windswept & rough, secluded & sunny
122	123	miles long, several entries, some calm enough
126	127	easiest snorkel in Kaua'i, tops for beginners
132	133	30-foot deep water, usually clear & protected
136	137	big sheltered beach, calmer than most, but few fish
142	145	snorkeling safest between Kawailoa & Gillen's, dunes
150	151	popular, small, boulder habitat, avoid if south swell
154	155	partially protected, room to explore, long beach
158	159	no beach, usually calm, partial protection, good variety
162	163	shallow entry, but good snorkeling, turtle hang-out
165	163	good variety, usually calm enough, semi-protected
174	175	usually very calm within reef, partial protection
182	179	remote, poor road, often too rough, uncrowded
190	191	back of volcanic crater, clear, excursion only, tops

Northwest Area

Picturesque beaches with a backdrop of towering mountains have made this lush, green corner of Kauaʻi the location of choice as a backdrop for many movies. From Kēʻē Beach at the far end of the road to Hanalei Bay, you'll find some of Kauaʻi's most beautiful scenery. Highway 56 narrows and becomes a two-lane road at Hanalei, then proceeds west as Highway 560 over seven one-lane bridges as it winds through the northwest to the rugged and impassible Nā Pali Coast.

The Hanalei to Hāʻena area is the quietest and least developed corner of Kauaʻi, where you'll find no big hotels, condos, golf courses or even supermarkets. The quiet little town of Hanalei has the only shopping in the area. You will find scattered homes near the narrow corridor of Highway 560 and plenty of sand beaches with extensive offshore reefs. Rains can be heavy here (to say the least) with nearly 500 inches falling up on top of Mount Waiʻaleʻale, sending hundreds of narrow waterfalls cascading down the mountains and toward the sea. Winter storms from the North Pacific bring huge waves to this area, so snorkeling is usually much better in the summer.

Conditions change often, so come prepared for any kind of seas. For a snorkeler, that means learning which beaches are likely to be safe and enjoyable. It also entails knowing that all water sports can

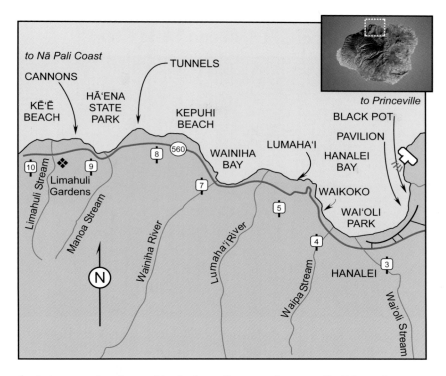

be interrupted quite suddenly by a fast-moving squall. Often, the heavy rains only last a few minutes and are quite warm, so these you can wait out. While heavy rain itself needn't bother a snorkeler, the brown run-off from the rivers after major downpours will certainly do a job on the visibility of the water. If steady rain settles in, you will prefer to snorkel elsewhere.

Kaua'i is a fairly small island, so this gorgeous area is easy to reach from all major tourist areas. The drive is green and relaxing: only ten miles from Princeville, half an hour from Kapa'a, and about an hour from Po'ipū (unless you hit rush hour traffic). Come when you have plenty of time to relax and enjoy the snorkeling as well as the many wonderful attractions, such as the Limahuli Botanical Gardens. No permit is required to hike the first stretch of the Kalalau Trail, and it makes a spectacular day hike.

Except for the Hanalei Colony Resort, the only accommodations available are in numerous private beach rental homes. Most of these are found on the ocean side (makai) of Highway 560. Renting one of these houses makes a great jungle vacation. Jungles have mosquitoes ants and other sometimes annoying critters, so bring repellent.

43

Kē'ē Beach (Hā'ena State Park)

We begin our tour of snorkeling sites with picturesque Kē'ē Beach, which is located at the far western end of Highway 560. No road can continue any further due to the rugged Nā Pali Coast. Come here for the scenic drive, the picture-perfect little cove with dramatic Mount Makana in the background, lush vegetation, and excellent snorkeling when seas are fairly calm. The small sandy beach is protected by an extensive reef, so is often calm when other nearby beaches are impossible. Both swimming and snorkeling are excellent here, entry is simple from the sand, and you'll find such beauty that you'll want to stay all day. The Kalalau Trail along the Nā Pali Coast begins here a few steps to the left of the beach. A short trail also leads from the beach to nearby terraces, and an old Hawai'ian hula heiau, where the views are nothing short of spectacular. We highly recommend Kē'ē Beach at any time of the year except after unusually heavy rains.

Novice snorkelers should stay within the sandy-bottomed bay taking care to stay well away from the deep channel on the left side of the bay, where currents can sweep you toward the Nā Pali Coast. Snorkeling is modest within the bay, but the beautiful setting and some bright reef fish will please most beginners.

More experienced snorkelers will prefer to explore over the shallow reef on the right side. When conditions permit (especially in the

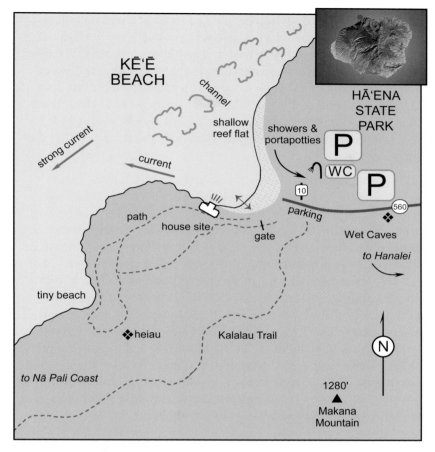

Map Symbols

Peak	▲	Location of picture	≋⌐|
Place of interest	❖		
Highway	━━━	Hotel or Condominium	H
Paved Road	─────	Parking area	P
Minor paved road	────		
Dirt Road	─·─·─·	Restroom	WC
Foot path	-------	Lava	🪨
Road Number	(50)	Sand	▨
Highway mileage marker	[11]	City	●

summer), you can skim the reef along a shallow channel on the right to the outer edge where turtles abound (see map above). High tide is the best time to come if you want to snorkel over the reef. The tides in Kauaʻi only swing about two feet, but it makes a big difference at this site. Low tide will give you only a claustrophobic one-foot clearance in spots, while high tide will usually provide about three feet. When large waves are crashing against the outer edge of the reef (more frequent in winter), all snorkelers should stay within the protected cove.

Kēʻē Beach is located within 230 acre Hāʻena State Park (not to be confused with nearby Hāʻena Beach Park). You'll find a large parking area, picnic spots, lifeguard, portapotties, and ever-present wild chickens. There's plenty of parking, but the park is getting very popular, so come early if you need to park within steps of the water. Plan to stay awhile and thoroughly enjoy this incredible beach. For a lovely short hike, take the trail at the left side of the beach, past an old building site and wander up to the heiau reputed to be the birthplace of Hawaiʻian hula. You'll need to cross over or around a short fence. It's a rocky trail and a bit steep, but not far. From the terraces you can look out on the Nā Pali Coast and back to the reef at Kēʻē Beach. An even steeper trail continues down to the next little beach west of Kēʻē, where you'll probably find no crowds at all. Do not swim or snorkel at this beach because a strong current sweeps to the left all along the coast beyond Kēʻē Beach.

The name Hāʻena means "red hot" and may have come from the ancient Hawaiʻian practice of throwing burning hollow sticks from the top of Mount Makana after dark. Look up and imagine what an enchanting sight it must have been to see "fireworks" raining down from the top of this steep mountain cloaked in greenery.

This enchanting and out-of-the-way corner of Kauaʻi was discovered by hippies in the ʻ70s, who gathered together on land owned by a brother of actress Liz Taylor. Strings of hippie-gathered puka shells created quite a fashion craze. Hawaiʻians of Niʻihau have continued this tradition, making some exquisite and expensive shell necklaces.

GETTING THERE
Kēʻē Beach, at the far end of the Kūhiō Highway, is one of the easiest to find. Simply follow Highway 56 until it becomes 560, then continue all the way to the end (at mile marker 10), where you're a stone's throw from the water. This is ten miles beyond Princeville (see maps, page 43 & 45).

As you pass Princeville and the highway winds down into the lush Hanalei Valley, it narrows to two lanes, crossing seven one-lane bridges where traffic must yield. Relax and enjoy the view if you're headed against the flow of traffic. This is Hawai'i, where drivers are usually courteous, so you'll get your turn in good time.

You will pass Hā'ena Beach Park on your right. Continue until you see the sign for Hā'ena State Park as you cross the Limahuli Stream, then park in one of the large dirt lots on your right. If you're feeling lucky, continue to the end of the road, where you may find a parking spot along the road just steps from the beach.

Just before entering the park, you will pass Limahuli Botanical Garden mauka (toward the mountains). You might want to stop here for a self-guided tour of one of the most beautiful tropical gardens in the world. It's best to call first for times and reservations.

Cannons (Hauwa)

Continuing in a clockwise direction, we come to Cannons (also called Hauwa), a broad reef extending from Kē'ē Beach in the west to Hā'ena Beach Park in the east. Most of the year this area is better for divers than snorkelers since the reef is shallow, the waves rough and the currents strong. It does provide arches and caves for the most experienced snorkeler. Entrance is possible from Kē'ē Beach to the west at high tide or from the sand at Hā'ena Beach Park to the east.

When surf is down and tide is up, the area nearest Kē'ē offers relatively safe snorkeling. Avoid the far north of this reef at all times because a gap in the center of the reef can cause a current out to where the offshore current, if strong, can easily sweep you toward the Nā Pali Coast.

Showers, restrooms, and picnic tables are all available at nearby Hā'ena Beach Park in the east and Kē'ē Beach in the west.

GETTING THERE   Park in the Hā'ena Beach Park makai (towards the water) Highway 560 at mile marker 9 (see map, page 49). Then, cross the sand to the left to snorkel the Cannons reef extending out from the western side of the beach.

Alternatively, park at Kē'ē Beach, then snorkel to the right across the reef. Continue to the right as far as Cannons only when conditions are very calm with high tide. You can usually catch the current to drift back to Kē'ē Beach.

Hā‘ena Beach Park (Maniniholo)

Easily confused with nearby Hā‘ena State Park (Kē‘ē Beach), Hā‘ena Beach Park is located a short drive to the east makai (towards the water) from Highway 560. The park offers camping, a broad sandy beach with a shallow stream, shower, restrooms, and picnic tables, so it's a handy spot to stop after a day at Kē‘ē or Tunnels. Parking is plentiful in the lot along the highway.

You can hike a quarter mile along the sand to your right (east) to get to Tunnels. There are closer entrances to Tunnels, but they usually fill very early in the day, so keep this parking area in mind. It's really not a long hike. Besides, at Hā‘ena Beach Park you'll have a shower waiting when you return from snorkeling. The shower is located inside that semi-shielded square area at the western end of the park.

Swimming is good at the park and you can snorkel here, but you'll find mostly sandy beach in the center, often with a strong current. In rough winter swells, the center can be particularly dangerous since it has no protecting reef directly in front. Snorkelers should definitely hike the quarter mile to Tunnels.

Along the highway, you'll find Wai‘akapala‘e and Wai‘akanaloa (Wet and Dry Caves). You might want to check them out while you're up in the area.

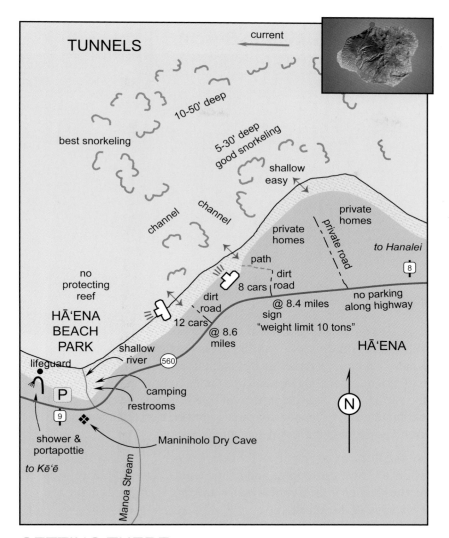

TUNNELS

current

10-50' deep

best snorkeling

5-30' deep
good snorkeling

shallow
easy

channel

channel

private
homes

private
homes

private road

to Hanalei

path

dirt
road

8

no
protecting
reef

dirt
road

8 cars

@ 8.4 miles
sign
"weight limit 10 tons"

no parking
along highway

HĀʻENA
BEACH
PARK

12 cars

@ 8.6
miles

HĀʻENA

shallow
river

560

lifeguard

P

camping

restrooms

N

9

shower &
portapottie

Maniniholo Dry Cave

to Kēʻē

Manoa Stream

GETTING THERE   Hāʻena Beach Park is located makai
(toward the ocean) Highway 560 at mile marker 9 (see map above).
You will see dirt parking areas along the highway, with camping and
picnicing nearby. Although the park is visible from the highway, it's
easy to drive right by without noticing it.

This is a low-key beach with visitors spread over about a half mile
of sand. While there is swimming in front, the better snorkeling entry
is at Tunnels, which requires a quarter-mile hike across sand to the
right. Snorkeling and swimming in front of Hāʻena Beach Park should
be limited to very calm seas because a strong current here pulls out
and to the left.

Tunnels (Makua Beach)

When surf is fairly low (very likely during the summer), Tunnels is Kaua'i's premier snorkeling destination. The large horseshoe-shaped reef has an outer edge that catches the pounding waves and delights the surfers. An extensive inner reef is available for easy snorkeling within the natural lagoon-like area — providing winter storm waves aren't pounding all the way to shore.

No facilities are available at Tunnels, but nearby Hā'ena Beach Park offers a shower, restrooms and picnic tables. There is plenty of space on the sand near the Tunnels reef with large shade trees along the back edge of the beach.

The most convenient parking for Tunnels is along either of the short entrance roads (see map, page 49), but both tend to fill early (7 a.m.). If you arrive later, you can park at Hā'ena Beach Park and walk a quarter mile to your right (east) on sand to get to the Tunnels area. Cross the river where it enters the sea and is only inches deep.

Snorkeling entries are easy from the wide sand beach, especially where we've marked on our map. Avoid the shallow areas with reef and rocks extending to the beach edge. Beginners should stay close to shore following the inner reef. Even in the best weather, there tends to be a slight current toward the left (west). Be careful not to drift too far. You can always enter further up the beach to the right and simply drift slowly along the reef and exit closer to the left edge of the reef. This inner area ranges from about three to thirty feet deep with channels, caverns and, yes, tunnels.

More experienced snorkelers will want to explore closer to the outer reef (depending on currents and swell). When calm enough, this reef has plenty of room to explore. In places it drops off to about 50-70 feet. The outer reef is our favorite. We've seen turtles, huge cornetfish, parrotfish, pearl wrasses, rockmover wrasses, big chubs and jacks, turtles, and even white-tipped reef sharks. All of these creatures can even be seen close to shore if you're lucky.

Tunnels is a must-see when the weather co-operates, but stay out of the water when huge waves cross the reef, which they often do in winter storms.

Note: there is a generic warning sign posted all year, as at many hotels these days, no matter what the conditions, so check out the ocean yourself before getting discouraged. We've talked to people who turned back after driving all the way to Tunnels and reading the sign (on a perfect day, no less). Just ignore the sign and walk another 100 yards to see for yourself what the day's conditions are like.

GETTING THERE
From Princeville, take Highway 560 (Kūhiō Highway) through the town of Hanalei, past Hanalei Bay and past the Hanalei Colony Resort. Watch the mile markers carefully if you want to park close to Tunnels.

There are three public accesses to Tunnels. The closest and coveted parking is found at the entrance at mile 8.4 where a short dirt road turns toward the beach (the sign here says "Weight limit 10 tons"). Parking is allowed on one side of this road only (about 8 cars). Take this dirt road half a block to the short palm-lined trail heading left from the end. Don't even think about blocking anyone's driveway access. Parking is no longer allowed anywhere along the main highway.

You'll also find a short dirt road from Highway 560 with parking for 12 cars at mile 8.6 if you watch for the mile markers. Divers come early for the best parking, so it fills by about 7 a.m.

Tunnels is also an easy quarter-mile walk along the sand from Hā‘ena Beach Park, where ample parking, restrooms, shower, and lifeguard are located. Park in the lot at mile marker 9 (see map, page 49), then wade across the shallow stream on the right and continue to hike across the sand to where the reef and fellow snorkelers will be easily visible.

Kepuhi Beach

This mile-long sandy beach has a broad fringing reef offshore with alternating sandy channels and reef. While not the calmest spot (a bit more exposed to surf than Tunnels), it can provide excellent snorkeling in favorable weather—especially in the summer. Direct access is blocked by the private homes along most of the beach, but Alamoʻo Road will get you to the sand. Snorkel out to the reef, which is close to shore, watching carefully that you don't get caught in any current to the left. Large winter swells from the north will make it impossible, but there's a wide reef area to explore when seas are calm. You'll find many of the same creatures here that are seen at Tunnels, but will seldom see other snorkelers.

GETTING THERE   Located to the ocean side (makai) of Highway 560, the reef is in front of private homes, so not very visible from the highway (see map, page 53). You will pass Wainiha Bay at mile marker 7, then Kepuhi Beach begins at the western point of Wainiha Bay and wraps around the corner toward the town of Hāʻena. Access is from Alamoʻo or ʻĀleʻaleʻa Roads, or by hiking from the highway or private homes. For the best snorkeling, drift left (west) toward Tunnels. The reef continues to the left edge of Tunnels.

Wainiha Bay

This is a lovely, uncrowded beach with a large lagoon just west of Lumahaʻi Beach. Since the Wainiha River flows in here, snorkeling isn't great, but it's a nice place for a swim when calm. There's a wide nearly deserted sandy beach near the highway Usually a large sand bar develops at the mouth of the river, but this sand moves around with the seasons.

Don't swim or snorkel here when north swell rolls in or heavy rain causes flooding and murky water. The Wainiha Valley drains from the beautiful 5,000 foot-high mountains in the background, so this river can rise quickly creating a flash flood.

Snorkeling is best around the point to the left, and gets better as you head toward Kepuhi and Tunnels. If you have a way to return, you can take a long, slow snorkel with the current ending just past Tunnels, where you will find a shower and restrooms.

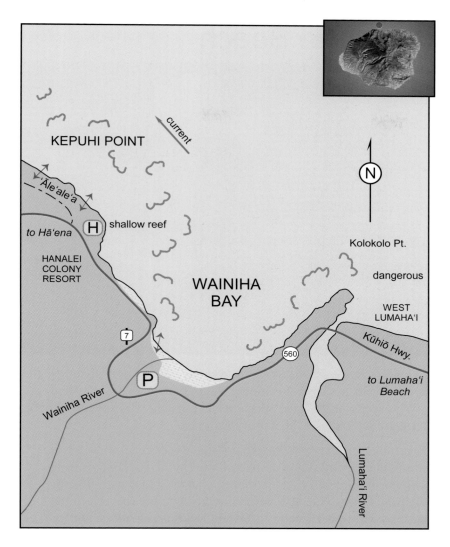

KEPUHI POINT

current

'Ale'ale'a

to Hā'ena

shallow reef

H

HANALEI COLONY RESORT

N

Kolokolo Pt.

dangerous

WEST LUMAHA'I

WAINIHA BAY

Kūhiō Hwy.

7

560

P

to Lumaha'i Beach

Wainiha River

Lumaha'i River

GETTING THERE

Wainiha Bay can be seen from Highway 560 (see map above). Parking is available in several spots along the road, and you'll have no crowds to worry about. Also no facilities. You'll find Wainiha just east of mile marker 7.

Lumaha'i Beach

Lumaha'i is one of Kaua'i's most famous beaches and one of its loveliest. Scenes from the movie "South Pacific" were shot here in 1957 and Mount Mākaha (close to Kē'ē Beach) was inserted into the background to create the illusory Bali Hai.

You can catch a view of the picturesque eastern end of the beach from the highway at one of the turn-outs along Highway 560. To swim or snorkel, hike down a short, relatively easy path from the highway through the lush vegetation to get to the east end of the beach. Parking is available at several locations along the highway. The path itself is easy to miss in the dense foliage, so watch carefully for the mileage (see map, page 55) or you'll likely sail on by.

Lumaha'i lacks the protecting reef of nearby beaches. Strong wave action on its shifting sands often creates a steeply sloped beach with a wicked undertow. When conditions are poor, Lumaha'i still offers a delightful spot for a picnic and is well worth the short hike. The beach is widest at the end of summer before winter storms move much of the sand.

When calm enough, the swimming is excellent at the far right, while body-surfers often play in the waves in front. Snorkeling at Lumaha'i

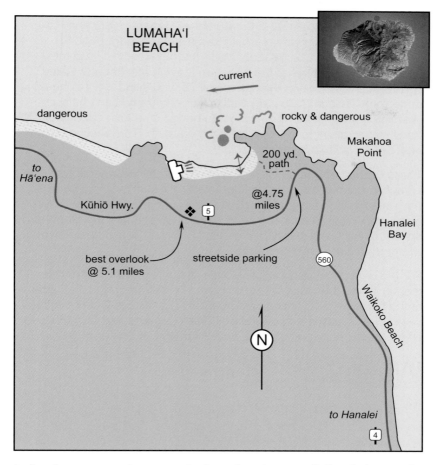

LUMAHA'I
BEACH

current

dangerous

rocky & dangerous

Makahoa
Point

200 yd.
path

to
Hā'ena

@4.75
miles

Hanalei
Bay

Kūhiō Hwy.

5

best overlook
@ 5.1 miles

streetside parking

560

Waikoko Beach

N

to Hanalei

4

is fun, but you won't see much since there's no reef. Snorkel around the rocks watching for some of the local reef fish.

When big swells are rolling in (common in the winter), be extremely cautious. The undertow can be worse than it looks due to the steep slope of the sand. Also, large sets of waves can arrive with no warning. Many have managed to drown themselves here (second only to Hanakāpī'ai along the Nā Pali Coast). These statistics include people who were swept off the rocks and others caught in flash floods in the river. No lifeguards are on duty and no facilities are available at Lumaha'i.

While you will find a steep path to the western end of Lumaha'i (previously called Kāhalahala for its hala trees), snorkeling or swimming anywhere except the far eastern end is too dangerous in any season.

GETTING THERE

Lumaha'i Beach is very easy to miss. Watch the highway markers carefully (see map, page 55). There are several little turnouts along the highway, but note mile marker 4 as you drive up the hill when leaving the Hanalei Valley. At a bend in the road at exactly mile 4.75, you'll find the trail heading down to the beach. This easy trail is unmarked and can't be seen until you get out of the car. The trail, shaded by a lush canopy of hala trees, winds down to the east end of the beach. This section is your best bet for swimming or snorkeling.

There is another trail further to the west, but the west section of Lumaha'i doesn't offer a safe spot to swim. Either trail can be slippery after heavy rains, which do happen suddenly and often in this green and lovely corner of Kaua'i. Most showers here are warm and end in minutes, but heavy rain can settle in and cause flash flooding where any rivers enter the sea.

For the best place to take that picture of Lumaha'i, watch for mile marker 5 and then take the next turnout on the ocean (makai) side of the highway. This spot would be mile 5.1 although it isn't marked in any way. There are several other small turnouts, but only this one offers the most commonly photographed view of Lumaha'i Beach.

Waikoko Beach

While this isn't the best snorkeling around, it's a lovely spot with broad sand beach. Located at the western end of two-mile long Hanalei Bay, Waikoko Beach offers a gentle slope to the sand and is never crowded. Snorkeling is best at the far left (northwest) corner of the beach, where there is some protection behind a natural reef breakwater. When calm enough, snorkeling is good all the way around the corner to the left. Swimming is best near the center.

Big swells from the north (common in the fall and winter) can render this beach dangerous, so check out the waves carefully. Sometimes Waikoko is the calmest beach along Hanalei Bay, IF the exact angle of the swells spares it. Though the slope of the sand will change with the seasons, Waikoko is usually fairly shallow. This makes it better for snorkeling than swimming even though there's a sandy bottom. Heavy rains (common here in northern Kaua'i) swiftly bring brown-water runoff from the river, ruling out any snorkeling.

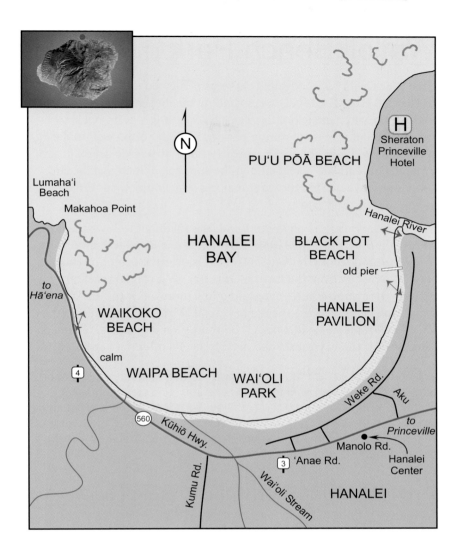

N

Lumaha'i Beach

Makahoa Point

PU'U PŌĀ BEACH

Sheraton Princeville Hotel

Hanalei River

HANALEI BAY

BLACK POT BEACH

old pier

to Hā'ena

WAIKOKO BEACH

HANALEI PAVILION

calm

4

WAIPA BEACH

WAI'OLI PARK

Weke Rd.

Aku

560 Kūhiō Hwy.

to Princeville

Manolo Rd.

Kumu Rd.

3 'Anae Rd.

Hanalei Center

Wai'oli Stream

HANALEI

GETTING THERE   On the far western end of Hanalei Bay, you'll find this pretty and uncrowded beach along of the highway. The beach can be seen as you pass the town of Hanalei heading west (see map above). There's a parking area makai of the highway near mile marker 4 and you'll find all facilities nearby at Wai'oli Beach Park.

Wai'oli Beach Park (Pine Trees)

This beach with restrooms and showers is located toward the center of Hanalei Bay. The lovely trees shading this beach are actually ironwoods, often mistaken for pines. Snorkeling is poor, but swimming is fine except during periods of high north swell in the winter. When calm, the water is nearly flat with a wide sandy beach great for little kids—especially in the summer. Winter swells can sometimes sweep right through, making it unavailable for either swimming or snorkeling.

Wai'oli Beach Park is on Weke Road (the road that follows the edge of Hanalei Bay.) Either Manolo Road or 'Anae Road will take you to Weke Road from Highway 560. This is near the center of Hanalei Bay only blocks from the town of Hanalei, so it can be reached quickly for a shower after snorkeling in a more isolated location. The name Hanalei means lei-shaped bay, so Wai'oli is the middle of the lei. Heavy rains make this beach too murky for snorkeling. Being in the center of the bay means that winter swells often hit hard here.

GETTING THERE   Wai'oli Beach Park is just two short blocks from the town of Hanalei (where you will see mile marker 3), but is well-hidden from the highway. Turn toward the bay on any street from the center of town and you'll find the park at the center of Hanalei Bay. It's located on Weke Road (see map, page 57). There's plenty of parking and all facilities.

Hanalei Pavilion Beach

While you'll find lifeguards and all facilities available here, the swimming and snorkeling aren't really great—especially when winter swells roll straight into the bay. The Hanalei River adds fresh water nearby, so visibility is low most of the year. Still, it's a popular spot and can be very calm when waves are low. When calm, children play happily in the shallow water lapping the sandy beach. Showers, restrooms, picnic tables and parking are all available here.

GETTING THERE   Hanalei Pavilion is another park located on Weke Road (between Wai'oli and Black Pot Beaches). See map, page 57. Just take any road from the city two short blocks toward the bay, then turn right on Weke Road and you will come to the pavilion.

Black Pot Beach

Popular with locals, Black Pot Beach is a gathering spot that stretches from the old Hanalei pier to the mouth of the Hanalei River. When calm, children enjoy the wide sand and shallow water. When winter swells roll in, this can be a dangerous spot. When that happens, sit on the sand and enjoy the gorgeous view of the mountains towering over the west end of the valley with waterfalls in abundance (perhaps as many as one hundred).

All facilities, including camping, showers, restrooms, picnic tables, boat launch and plenty of parking are available here. There's lots of sand, but the beach is all fairly shallow. Since the Hanalei River pours into the bay here, visibility will be poor most of the time, making it better for splashing than snorkeling.

Dedicated snorkelers might want to swim across the Hanalei River and snorkel near Puʻu Pōā beaches. While it's a long swim, you might prefer the swim to climbing down Puʻu Pōā's 171 steps. Also, there's no parking problem at Black Pot Beach.

GETTING THERE

Black Pot is the beach at the far east of Hanalei Bay where the Hanalei River enters the bay (see map, page 57). It's located at the far northeastern end of Weke Road and hard to miss. You'll find ample parking and all facilities here. From Highway 560, just turn toward the ocean anywhere in the town of Hanalei, then right on Weke Road to the east.

Mel Malinowski

bannerfish

Princeville Area

Princeville, a planned community located on a bluff overlooking the north coast of Kauaʻi, is packed with hotels, condos, timeshares, restaurants, and homes. You'll find a golf course, supermarket, public library, and shopping, all in the center of Princeville, near the main entrance from Highway 56 at Ka Haku Road.

Beaches here are all located about two hundred feet below the steep bluff. Views are outstanding up on top, but snorkeling requires a hike. Some of the paths are relatively easy, while others require a difficult (sometimes slippery and treacherous) scramble down the cliff. Because of the climb (not to mention the dearth of public parking), most Princeville beaches are uncrowded and you might even have one to yourself, especially very early or late in the day.

Snorkeling, as well as swimming, can range from very easy in flat water to impossible when huge winter swells arrive from the north. Heavy rains can sometimes make most of the trails impassable. Still, when conditions are good (more often in the summer), these beaches are beautiful and mostly secluded. An offshore reef wraps much, but not all, of this northern area. Turtles abound along the cliffs and you might even see baby turtles in the natural salt-water swimming pool called Queen Emma's Bath.

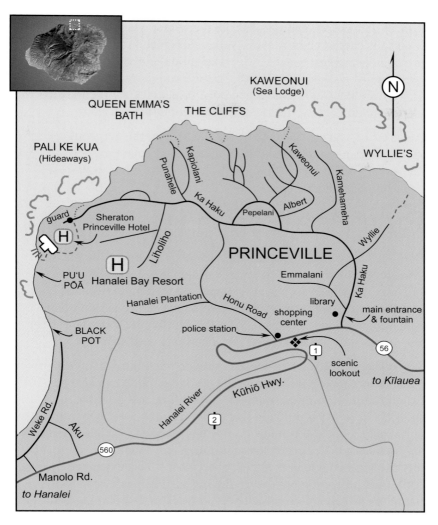

Even if you're staying in Princeville itself, parking is a serious problem. It's hard to understand why Princeville has chosen to provide so little visitor parking—since many of the folks wanting to enjoy these beaches may be staying elsewhere in Princeville. They penalize all of their guests in order to exclude a few visitors. We hope they'll adjust their attitude about this. But for the time being, come VERY early if you want the best chance to park and enjoy one of the little Princeville beaches. When the few ten-car public parking lots fill, all the other available parking lots are private and sport prominent tow-away signs (though we doubt they're quick to tow). Hotel parking is available though for dining or shopping.

Princeville is green and gorgeous in the winter when hundreds of waterfalls cascade into Hanalei Valley. Summer and fall usually provide the calmest beaches for water sports here. At times, the north can be calmer than Po'ipū, because summer swells tend to arrive from the south. We've listed the Princeville snorkeling sites in clockwise order as we follow the coast around Kaua'i.

Pause while you snorkel, float easy and soak in the gorgeous views looking out to sea and back toward the mountains beyond the Hanalei Valley. You'll be glad you made the effort to discover Princeville's secluded coves.

Pu'u Pōā Beach (Princeville Hotel)

Pu'u Pōā's two small beaches are located down below the Sheraton Princeville Hotel (only 171 concrete steps). Since all of the Princeville beaches are about two hundred feet down from the bluff, you'll need to hike to get to the water, so the choice is steps, slippery path, ramp or dangerous path. Pu'u Pōā and Wyllie's are the easiest and safest—steps at Pu'u Pōā and a ramping path at Wyllie's.

While Hanalei Bay can be closed out with huge breakers when winter storm swells roll in from the north Pacific, it can also be bathtub calm most of the summer. At that time, it's possible to snorkel out from Pu'u Pōā in five to ten feet of water, then to the north and around the bend to several tiny isolated beaches. In some ways this is a better beach for snorkeling than swimming: there are reef patches and boulders almost everywhere. This extensive fringing reef offers protection only when the big surfing waves stay away. Summer and fall are far more likely to be calm, but nothing is for sure when you're predicting Kaua'i's weather, where swells from far across the Pacific can arrive at any time.

While this isn't the best snorkeling beach in northern Kaua'i, and isn't usually very clear, there's still enough to see if you take the time and wander. Once we happened upon a couple of white-tipped reef sharks close to the beach in about ten feet of water. You won't see great coral here or a lot of fish, but you're almost certain to see turtles if you stay out for awhile. They're abundant along the cliffs as you snorkel along the coast to the north. When swells permit, stop to visit one of the tiny isolated sandy coves along the base of the cliff. Even if you can't swim here, the view of mountains and waterfalls is just gorgeous.

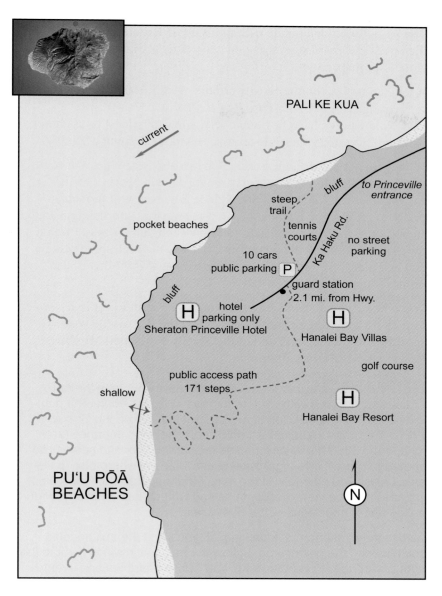

current

PALI KE KUA

bluff

steep trail

to Princeville entrance

pocket beaches

tennis courts

Ka Haku Rd.

no street parking

10 cars
public parking P

guard station
2.1 mi. from Hwy.

bluff

H hotel
parking only
Sheraton Princeville Hotel

H
Hanalei Bay Villas

golf course

public access path
171 steps

shallow

H
Hanalei Bay Resort

PU'U PŌĀ
BEACHES

N

The partially-hidden public path to Puʻu Pōā Beaches begins just to the left of the guard station as you approach the Sheraton Princeville Hotel (see map, page 63).

A ten-car parking lot makai (toward the ocean) from the path provides parking for both Puʻu Pōā and Pali Ke Kua IF you're very early or very lucky. Alternatively, you can request to use hotel parking for various plausible reasons, such as shopping or dining.

When you get down to the beach, you can also scramble over some rocks on the left to get to a nearly-empty second beach. This is easiest when the tide is low. Snorkelers, however, will probably prefer to enter from the main beach since the best snorkeling is to the right (north). Entry is easy here from the sand, but it pays to watch for rocks. Coral isn't abundant here, but you may see some pelagic fish and plenty of turtles. The boulder habitat at Puʻu Pōā is also prime octopus territory.

When huge winter swells hit hard, you won't want to get in the water for either swimming or snorkeling. Ask at the Princeville water sports office (at the north end of the beach) if in doubt. Mornings tend to be calmer than afternoons.

GETTING THERE

From Highway 56, take the main Princeville entrance with the fountain, on Ka Haku Road. The public access parking lot is found on the right just before the Sheraton Princeville guard station at 2.1 miles from the main entrance (see map, page 63). This small lot holds ten cars at best and serves two beaches. There's little legal parking available anywhere else in the area unless you plan to visit the hotel for shopping, lunch, or a bit of sightseeing. The view of mountains and waterfalls is definitely worth a stop and is spectacular after heavy rain.

Across the street from this parking lot, you'll find the trail heading south toward the golf course. Follow the trail until it winds back to the right toward the Princeville Hotel. You'll pass their pool and eventually arrive at the beach. There are two beaches here, but the best entry for snorkeling is just to the right of where the path emerges on the sand. The other beach is located out of sight to the left and can be reached if the tide isn't too high.

Some people park along the service road at the south of the hotel and walk down the ramped dirt road to avoid the many steps. However, it's possible this would get your car towed.

feather duster worm

Pali Ke Kua Beach (Hideaways)

These two secluded beaches are also called Hideaways or, less often, Kenomene. Located between the Princeville Hotel and the Pali Ke Kua condos, the Pali Ke Kua beaches offer snorkeling when conditions are relatively calm—especially in the summer. They have broad shallow areas near shore, making both beaches poor swimming destinations. In fact, even snorkeling is best at high tide. The sand beaches vary with the seasons, so you're likely to find them most appealing prior to the winter swells.

Access requires hiking down about two hundred feet from the road from two separate locations. Once down to the beach, you can snorkel from one to the other IF calm enough that swells won't slap you against the coral or rocks. When extra calm, advanced snorkelers can roam outside the fringing reef.

When conditions are favorable, the best snorkeling is at the far right end in a tiny protected area tucked into the eastern point. The snorkeling here is calmer, deeper and a bit more clear. While the private ramp at northeast end provides much easier hiking, you will have to scramble over a boulder area to get to the water. For public access, you must hike (often scramble and slide) down to the beach at the southwest end.

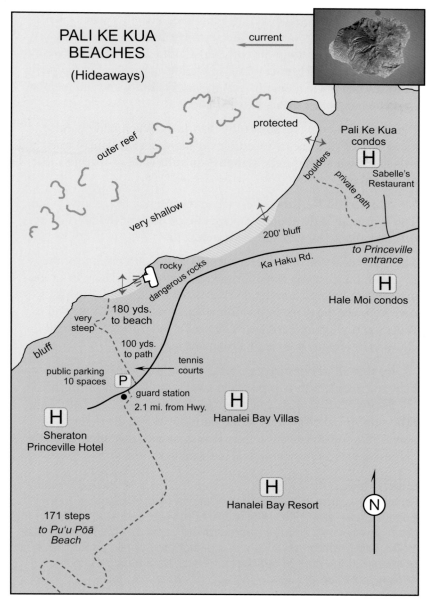

PALI KE KUA BEACHES

(Hideaways)

current

outer reef

protected

Pali Ke Kua condos

H

Sabelle's Restaurant

private path

boulders

very shallow

200' bluff

to Princeville entrance

Ka Haku Rd.

rocky

dangerous rocks

H

Hale Moi condos

180 yds. to beach

very steep

bluff

100 yds. to path

tennis courts

public parking 10 spaces

P

guard station 2.1 mi. from Hwy.

H

Hanalei Bay Villas

H

Sheraton Princeville Hotel

171 steps to Pu'u Pōā Beach

H

Hanalei Bay Resort

N

There are only ten designated parking spaces at the start of the trail — with no other legal parking nearby. The hike is fairly difficult over rocks and the swim is over some shallow reef. All in all, access to Pali Ke Kua is challenging, especially after wet weather. A rope strung along the side of the path where it's steepest provides some much-needed security.

Most of the Pali Ke Kua reef area has poor visibility when swells roll in from the north, but we did see huge schools of tangs (many hundreds) grazing along the reef. Most of the reef is five to twenty feet deep. The reef further offshore has lots of turtles, but the poor visibility can make them difficult to see. Visibility and fun greatly improve here when seas are extra calm.

If not so calm, you can still enjoy the lovely beach with its false kamani trees (the ones with edible nuts looking like Brazil nuts) and hala trees that appear to be standing on stilts (one of world's most ancient trees).

The trail to Pali Ke Kua is best when completely dry, which is rare. You'll need to walk about 100 yards to the edge of the bluff, then descend about 180 yards to the beach below.

The hike takes you down steep steps with a guard railing for the first half, then a steep slope for the rest of the way. There is a rope available to help assure you don't slide down the path. This is definitely not the place to go after a heavy rain because the soil in Kaua'i gets slippery very fast. The trail is too difficult for small children or anyone who isn't strong and steady.

Notice that all of our maps are arranged so that north is up. This will help you decide where to go when swells roll in from storms across the Pacific. Pali Ke Kua catches the full north swell, except for the little semi-protected corner at the far right. While the outer reef here offers some protection from waves, it isn't enough to keep the biggest waves from washing all the way to shore.

GETTING THERE

From Highway 56, take the main Princeville entrance (with fountain) on Ka Haku Road toward the ocean. Curve along Ka Haku to the northwest and at 2.1 miles from the highway you'll see the guard station for the Sheraton Princeville Hotel. Park here on your right in a designated public parking lot that holds about ten cars at best. A small sign here indicates "public access to beach."

This one public lot serves Pali Ke Kua as well as Pu'u Pōā, and there's virtually no alternative parking available, so come very early to find a space (before 8 a.m.). The public trail to Pali Ke Kua heads toward the ocean (while the trail across the street heads mauka toward Pu'u Pōā). You'll need to walk the narrow path between the parking lot and the Pu'u Pōā tennis courts, then pass the pool, 100 yards to get to the trail at the edge of the bluff (see map, page 69).

Here you'll find steps with a railing for the first half, then a security rope for the next half. This trail (100 yards) is way too slippery after a heavy rain (more like a water slide) and requires caution at all times because it's extremely steep.

After reaching the beach, to snorkel you may want to continue to the section further to the right. If so, you'll have to scramble over boulders that separate these two beaches. Avoid trying to hike further up the slope.

If you happen to be staying in the Pali Ke Kua condos (Sabelle's Restaurant turnoff), there's a asphalt path available just inside the condo entrance that is fairly steep, but much safer. Signs here warn "private" and "tow-away zone." A scramble over boulders awaits at the bottom.

Off to the far right of the beaches is a pretty little area that is somewhat protected by the point curving in. The water here is about 5-20' deep and can be clearer than the rest of the beach.

There are no facilities near Pali Ke Kua—just sand and shade. From the makai side of Ka Haku Road, you can get an excellent view of both beaches.

underside of crown of thorns seastar

Queen Emma's Bath

One of our sentimental favorites. While requiring a hike down about two hundred feet from the Princeville plateau at the end of Punahele Road, this natural saltwater swimming pool (complete with fish and coral) is well worth the effort. Check our map (page 71) because it's hard to find. Don't be discouraged too early because you won't see it until you round a corner, and there it is!

Parking is limited to about ten marked spaces, so come early (usually before 8 a.m.) to find parking. You'll also enjoy the enchanting pool without crowds. High storm surf sometimes makes the pool unsafe in the winter, but smaller waves won't reach it.

This is a unique and beautiful spot. Besides snorkeling and swimming, you can look out across the Hanalei Valley to the dramatic mountains in the distance. Incoming salt water often forms a waterfall at the north end of the pool, while waves sometimes splash into the middle filling the pool with bubbles. Low tide sometimes leaves the pool low, so we prefer high tide, especially for the jacuzzi action. When waves are high enough (especially sudden winter swells), it can be dangerous. In fact, you could be swept out to sea, as happened to one man a few years ago. If in doubt, steer clear!

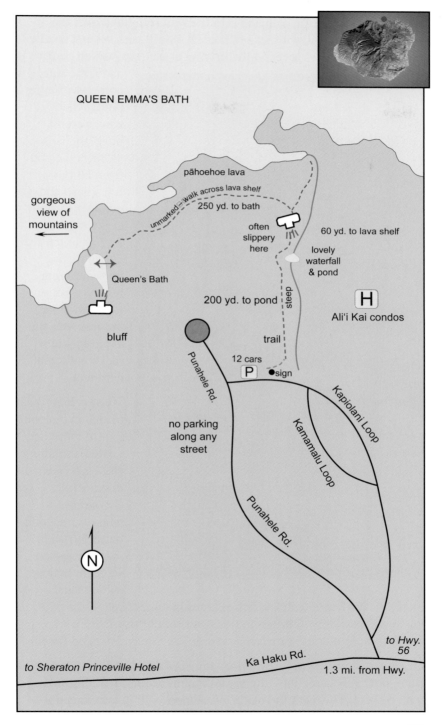

QUEEN EMMA'S BATH

gorgeous
view of
mountains

pāhoehoe lava

unmarked — walk across lava shelf

250 yd. to bath

often
slippery
here

60 yd. to lava shelf

lovely
waterfall
& pond

Queen's Bath

200 yd. to pond

steep

H

Ali'i Kai condos

bluff

trail

Punahele Rd.

12 cars

P

●sign

Kapiolani Loop

no parking
along any
street

Kamamalu Loop

Punahele Rd.

N

to Hwy.
56

to Sheraton Princeville Hotel

Ka Haku Rd.

1.3 mi. from Hwy.

71

After hiking down the path and past the waterfall, then over the smooth (pāhoehoe) lava rocks to the left, you'll pass several smaller pools and tiny coves, eventually arriving at the lava-walled pool

about the size of a home swimming pool. When waves aren't huge, the lava protects the pool from all but a fun splash and a gentle waterfall at the north end. At five to ten feet deep, it's fine for swimming, but even better for snorkeling, because you can avoid kicking rocks with your bare feet.

We saw hundreds of fish in the pool the first time we visited, including close-up views of colorful Christmas wrasses, raccoon butterflyfish, saddle wrasses, sergeant majors, and unusual blennies. We hear that baby turtles are sometimes seen in the pool. On another visit, with different tides and water flow, there were fewer fish, so it does seem to vary from day to day. No need for fins!

Of course, there are no facilities of any kind down at Queen Emma's Bath, not even sand. Only the natural bubble bath. Treat this area with respect. This isn't the place for cannon-balling into the pool.

GETTING THERE

Limited public parking is available for Queen Emma's Bath. None is available along side streets. The ten spaces (between the little blue signs) fill quite early — leaving no other legal place to park, so come very early in the day or late afternoon. Keep in mind that darkness settles rapidly in Kaua'i, so head back out in time to hike while it's still light.

From the main Princeville entrance (with fountain) on Highway 56, take Ka Haku Road exactly 1.4 miles (see map, page 71), then turn makai (right) on Punahele Road where there is no longer a street sign. Follow Punahele for .3 mile north where you will see the parking where Punahele and Kapi'olani converge for a second time (see map, page 69). The path, located to the right of the parking, winds down the bluff 200 yards to a pretty waterfall and small pond on your right. Another 60 yards gets you to the rocks near the water. At this point, walk left on fairly flat and smooth pāhoehoe lava. Continue 250 yards past a number of tiny pools and a couple of bays until you come upon the Queen Emma's Bath, which is completely enclosed with wave splash flowing in at the far north and out at the southwest. It's about the size of a large backyard swimming pool.

This is the end of the hike, so you can't miss it as long as you go far enough. From Queen Emma's Bath, you'll be able to look back at the spectacular mountain range beyond Hanalei Valley — something you won't see until you reach this point.

yellowmargin surgeonfish

The Cliffs

If staying in Princeville and you happen to find the ocean perfectly calm, you might be tempted to try the path down the cliff at the far north. However, there's no beach here, the cliff is steep, and entry is only possible from the lava rocks. This is definitely not for a beginner, but the water can be clear and turtles abundant. We've seen it calm as bath water, which is what you need to enter the water from rocks in the north. This is for advanced snorkelers only due to changeable conditions, which could make your exit challenging. From the top of the bluff, you're likely to see turtles grazing along the rocks—especially in the late afternoon.

GETTING THERE   It's best to be staying at or near the Cliff's Resort in Princeville, since no public parking is provided. The trail down from their property is marked at the edge of the bluff with a discouraging sign. It is steep and can be dangerous when slippery. Take great care when entering the water from lava and watch that swells aren't picking up. Snorkel along the cliff in either direction watching carefully to find your exit later. Leave something bright to mark the spot where you enter the water because this isn't the place to get lost.

Mel Malinowski

Picasso (lagoon) triggerfish

Kaweonui Beach (Sea Lodge)

Kaweonui (also called Sea Lodge Beach, after the name of the condo just up the bluff) is difficult to find and offers no public parking, but this is one of our favorites. Even guests at Princeville may have a hard time finding the way. You can check our map (page 77) for the location of the trail that heads from the north Princeville cliff down to the beach. This quarter-mile jungle trail itself is beautiful under lush false kamani, hala and other tropical trees with birds singing in the canopy.

The path is narrow, but maintained, tucked in the shade of ironwoods. There are some fairly steep spots, so avoid this trail after a heavy rain, which would make the path quite slippery. Go slow and enjoy the beauty of this trail lined with sweet-smelling wild guava. At the bottom, you will need to hike over some rocks, but not for far—only about one hundred feet.

The small beach has coarse sand and deep shade and is usually empty. The inner bay is too shallow for swimming, but excellent for snorkeling when swell is low. Winter often brings big waves from the north and low tide will provide poor clearance, so choose your time carefully. Tides in Hawai'i only vary by about two feet, but at

Kaweonui that means the difference between one-foot clearance and three as you skim the reef to the outer wall. While the inner area is fairly protected by outer reef, don't take chances in a shallow site like this if there's any possibility of larger sets that could mash you on the rocks or coral. Even the sandy beach is unsafe in the most severe winter storms.

We enter on the right side of the beach (see map, page 77) in a small channel that angles to the right out of the shallowest area. Then snorkel left across the shallow reef to explore the outer edge where the water is six to twenty feet deep—perfect for snorkeling. Skimming over the shallow reef, we saw a large octopus at close range just feet from the sand. Larger fish were darting about in the crevices (about five feet below the reef surface). Outside the edge of the reef, parrotfish, turtles, and pelagic fish were everywhere in about twenty feet of water.

GETTING THERE

Kaweonui (commonly called Sea Lodge Beach for the condos up on top) has no public parking and can be difficult to find. You can park elsewhere and walk in from wherever you find parking, or stay in one of Princeville's many condos and hike to the start of the trail.

From the main entrance to Princeville (with the fountain), take Ka Haku Road for .7 mile, then turn right on Kamehameha Road. At .3 mile at the Y, go left toward Sea Lodge condos, rather than right to Kamehameha condos. Continue to the end of the road.

The quarter-mile path starts after you walk between the Sea Lodge condos labeled B and C (see map, page 77). You'll immediately come to a sign marked "section A." Walk across the grass, holding to the left for about one hundred yards toward the bluff. At the bluff, you'll see a sign, where the steep trail heads down though the trees to the beach at the bottom of the bluff. This trail will be quite slippery after a heavy rain and requires caution at all times.

Go about one hundred yards until you cross a small creek, then head left on the inland trail rather than taking the faint trail to the right. The trail is fairly well-maintained, but steep. Proceed another 200 yards emerging at Kaweonui Beach, a small sand beach tucked to the left of the point, which offers some protection from surf. Check our map for the best snorkeling entry point at the right, where you will find a narrow channel (of sorts) through the reef. This will get you to the far edge of the large fringing reef running all the way to and across 'Anini Beach. Large winter waves can sweep across this protecting reef all the way across the beach, so stay away in bad weather.

76

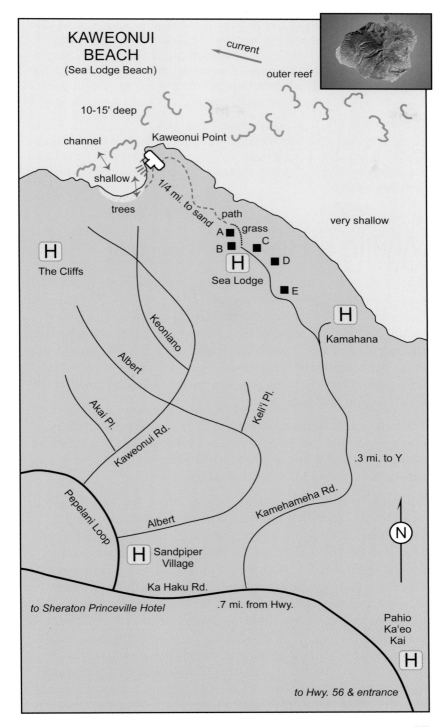

KAWEONUI
BEACH
(Sea Lodge Beach)

current

outer reef

10-15' deep

channel

Kaweonui Point

shallow

trees

1/4 mi. to sand

path

A

grass

B

C

very shallow

H

The Cliffs

H
Sea Lodge

D

E

Keoniano

H

Albert

Kamahana

Akai Pl.

Keli'i Pl.

Kaweonui Rd.

.3 mi. to Y

Pepelani Loop

Kamehameha Rd.

Albert

N

H
Sandpiper
Village

Ka Haku Rd.

to Sheraton Princeville Hotel

.7 mi. from Hwy.

Pahio
Ka'eo
Kai

H

to Hwy. 56 & entrance

With calm weather and a high tide, it's a delightful spot. Follow the narrow sandy "channel" that angles to the right (see map, page 77), then take a left turn when you have enough clearance and cross over the reef to the outer edge. Snorkel in either direction along the far edge of the reef, but do remember to note the channel location in order to return to the same spot for exit.

Low tide won't provide quite enough clearance at the entry point, so be sure to check the tide tables if you want to snorkel at Kaweonui Beach. Bring your wetsuit too if you have one. Beginners may find the reef here a bit too claustrophobic, but experienced snorkelers will love this beach.

Wyllie's Beach (Puamana)

Wyllie's Beach, at the far eastern end of Princeville, requires a fairly easy .3 mile hike down the overgrown remnants of an old ranch road flanked by two rows of canopy trees (really a road turning into a gully). No stairs are required here, but the trail ramps enough to be slippery after a heavy rain. It's a picturesque walk with birds singing in the trees, well worth hiking even if you don't plan to get in the water. You'll see wild mangoes, fern-covered boulders, and a small waterfall along the path.

The trail is well-hidden. Although there is no designated parking, it's easy to find a spot along the side of the road. Just avoid parking in any of the condo lots, where you risk being towed. Access may change if the grassy bluff ever sprouts more condos.

We weren't very impressed with the snorkeling, but it's a beautiful small beach, completely empty, and quite calm as long as huge swells aren't rolling in from the north. High tide is essential if you plan to snorkel here and want any clearance between your body and the sharp coral. Wyllie's is really too shallow for swimming. This broad flat expanse of coral is located just to the west of the 'Anini River. Stay well to the left to avoid any current near the river. Snorkel anywhere within the shallow area. There isn't a lot to see, but you might spot an octopus. You'll sometimes see locals hunting here with spear guns when the tide is high and surf is low, so don't be surprised to see the octopuses do their best to disguise themselves—and their best is VERY impressive because they can instantly change both color and texture.

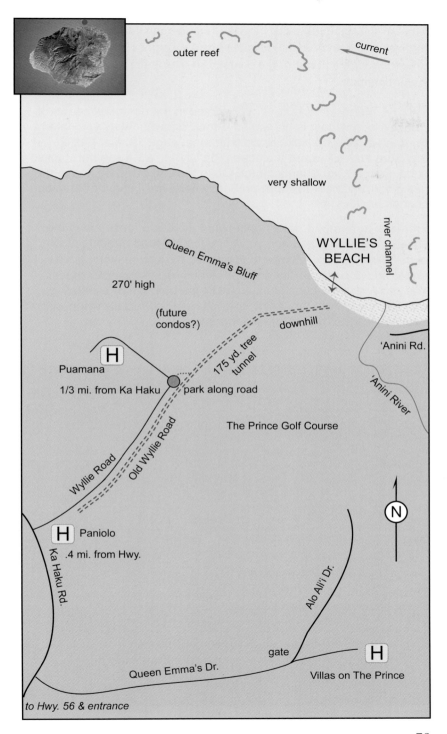

outer reef

current

very shallow

Queen Emma's Bluff

270' high

WYLLIE'S
BEACH

river channel

(future
condos?)

downhill

'Anini Rd.

175 yd. tree tunnel

Puamana

park along road

1/3 mi. from Ka Haku

'Anini River

Wyllie Road

Old Wyllie Road

The Prince Golf Course

H Paniolo

.4 mi. from Hwy.

Ka Haku Rd.

N

Alo Ali'i Dr.

gate

H

Queen Emma's Dr.

Villas on The Prince

to Hwy. 56 & entrance

Most of the surf will break far out along the outer edge of the reef, but higher breakers in the distance bring stronger currents pulling toward the left and out of the channels—particularly the main 'Anini River channel.

GETTING THERE

Located in the northeast corner of Princeville, this path is unmarked. From Highway 56 as you enter Princeville, take Ka Haku Road (see map, page 79) for .4 mile, then turn makai (toward the ocean) on Wyllie. You'll see the Paniolo condos on the right-hand corner. Go to the end of Wyllie and park along the road near this turn-around, where you'll see the Puamana condos on your left.

From the turnaround, walk right toward the line of trees along the edge of the golf course and you'll find the old road ramping down to the water—about .3 mile to the water. It's just one long gradual slope, and doesn't require any dangerous rock hopping or stairs. You can't miss the beach at the end of the trail. When snorkeling, stay left, away from the 'Anini River channel, especially when winter swells make the river channel dangerous.

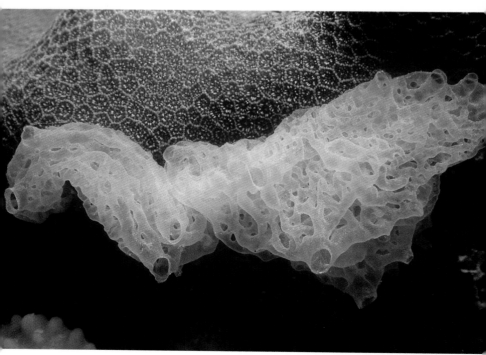

clathrina sponge

Snuba

Snuba® was developed as a simpler alternative to Scuba for shallow dives in resort conditions. Because Snuba divers are strictly limited in depth and conditions, and are always accompanied by a guide, the orientation takes just 15-30 minutes.

Two people share a small inflatable raft, which holds a Scuba air tank. A twenty-foot hose leads from the tank to a light harness on each diver. A comfortable weight belt completes your outfit. Very light and tropical!

Once in the water, your guide teaches you to breathe through your regulator (which has a mouthpiece just like your snorkel) on the surface until you're completely comfortable. You're then free to swim around as you like, remembering to clear your ears as needed (limited by the hose to twenty feet deep, of course).

The raft will automatically follow you as you tour the reef. It's that easy! You have to be at least eight years old, and have normal good health. Kids do amazingly well, and senior citizens can also enjoy Snuba. There's even a new program called Snuba Doo® for four to seven-year-old children. They wear a flotation vest, and breathe through a regulator as they float on the surface while their parents Snuba below.

We are certified Scuba divers, yet we often enjoy Snuba more. Less gear equals more fun. Snuba is a lot like snorkeling, with the added freedom to get down close to fish and coral. We often surface dive to check out what fish is hiding under a coral head. Snuba is like surface diving without having to come up for air!

Snuba provides a fun and safe experience if you pay attention and do it as directed. Their safety record is superb.

Warning: do pay attention to the instructions because even at these shallow depths, you must know the proper way to surface. You must remember to never hold your breath as you ascend or you could force a bubble of air into your blood. Breathing out continually while surfacing is not intuitive, but is absolutely necessary when you're breathing compressed air. This is especially important to remember if you're used to surface diving where you always hold your breath. Dive safely!

Northeast Area

Continuing clockwise around the island, we come to the northeast area between Princeville and Kīlauea, where you'll find several very long and broad sand beaches. Conditions vary with the weather, so you can't always count on calm water (especially in the fall and winter). Still, the beaches are lovely, uncrowded, and offer plenty of room to explore, both above and below the water.

When the tide is high, 'Anini Beach offers the longest inner protected lagoon in Kaua'i. A two-mile long reef far offshore protects the lagoon from the heavy breakers that crash against this reef most of the year. A beach park offers all amenities right along the water with plenty of space for snorkelers to wander in either direction within the inner lagoon.

Kauapea (Secret Beach) requires a moderate hike down through a ravine, but offers an excellent and secluded mile-long beach, although no facilities are available here. While often too rough for safe snorkeling or swimming, it's still pretty enough to be worth a visit. The west end of Kauapea also offers large tidepools to explore and take a dip. Small waterfalls provide an opportunity to rinse off at the base of the cliff.

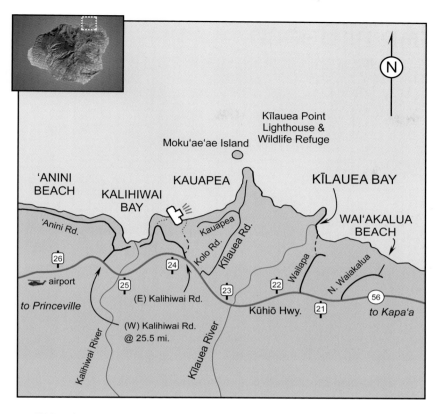

Kalihiwai Bay can be reached by car and offers a bit more protection from swells. Kayaking is popular here, both up the river and out to sea. Swimming and body-surfing are also popular at Kalihiwai.

Kīlauea Bay, further to the east, requires only a short hike, but most of the year catches the heavy northeastern swells making it far better for surfing than snorkeling.

With no hotels or condos in this less-developed northeast area, accommodations are located entirely in private homes. Many of these are found along 'Anini Road near the water. A few are located high above Kauapea with lovely broad views. Look for the rental signs or browse the internet. This is a beautiful section of the island, assuming you don't mind a little rain sometime during the day.

The big beaches of the northeast are often more popular for other water sports, such as windsurfing, surfing, kayaking, fishing, and the latest craze, kite-surfing. Come to 'Anini Beach when the wind is up (around three to four in the afternoon) to watch the kite-surfing.

'Anini Beach

This miles-long beach (called Wanini, Manini, Kalihiwai, or Kalihikai on some maps) has miles of protected reef to explore. The tidepools and tiny coves at the far east offer private little beaches. The center has a large public park with showers, restrooms, picnic tables, barbecues, camping, grass, boat launch, and ample parking. It's a popular destination for windsurfing, kayaking, and more recently kite-surfing. 'Anini Beach is almost entirely protected by an outer reef that catches the north waves. Many beach access paths are also located between private homes that front 'Anini Road.

The inner area where you can snorkel is huge, but shallow and not particularly interesting. The coral is largely covered with brown algae, so you have to swim awhile to see much. There are some spots with a bit of coral and fish, but mostly out toward the reef edge or along any of the channels.

When the sea is calm and tide is high, snorkeling here is easy with a distinct drift to the left. Our preference is to enter the water to the right (see map, page 85) and drift along through a couple of miles of shallow reef (checking out channels along the way), then hike back to the car. Somewhere along the line you're likely to spot turtles in

'ANINI BEACH

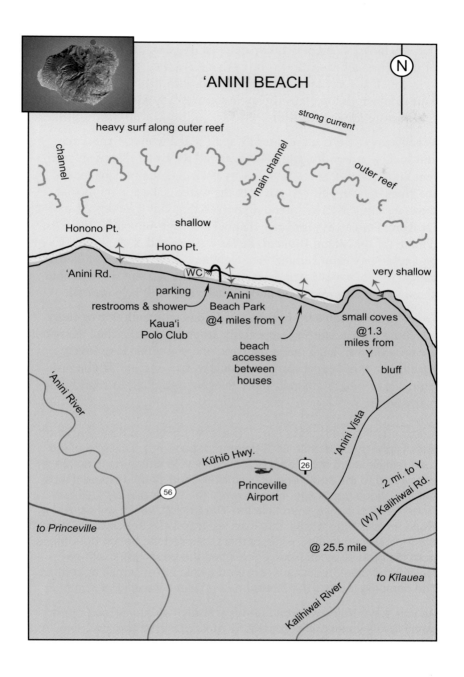

N

strong current

heavy surf along outer reef

channel

main channel

outer reef

shallow

Honono Pt.

Hono Pt.

'Anini Rd.

WC

very shallow

parking

restrooms & shower

'Anini
Beach Park
@4 miles from Y

small coves
@1.3
miles from
Y

Kaua'i
Polo Club

beach
accesses
between
houses

bluff

'Anini River

'Anini Vista

Kūhiō Hwy.

26

56

Princeville
Airport

.2 mi. to Y

(W) Kalihiwai Rd.

to Princeville

@ 25.5 mile

to Kīlauea

Kalihiwai River

deeper channels and perhaps an octopus in the shallows. While most of the inner reef is shallow (one to five feet), the channels drop off to as much as forty feet deep as they approach the outer barrier reef. Low tide here is too claustrophobic for most snorkelers, so check the tides before driving to 'Anini.

When heavy swells hit northern Kaua'i in the winter, 'Anini may still look wonderfully calm. However, all the water that pours over that far outer reef has to find its way back eventually. This means the channels can pull you out with the water. Take a good look at those distant waves and remind yourself that you'd rather not snorkel IN them. Stay away from any channel that tugs outward. This goes double for the 'Anini River at the far western end of the beach. Even on a relatively calm summer day we witnessed a rescue of a family caught in the waves when their kayak overturned and was swept to shore, while they remained in the break zone until help arrived.

Give 'Anini Beach a try in calm conditions with high tide or enjoy watching the kite-surfing (especially around 3-4 p.m. when the winds are up). Shower, hang out at the park, and enjoy this long lovely beach. Just don't expect large amounts of fish or coral. If you just want a lazy snorkel, there is more than enough space to snorkel for many hours.

GETTING THERE

The west section of Kalihiwai Road exits Highway 56 at mile 25.5 (see map, page 85). This end of the road, which is 2.5 miles east of the Princeville entrance, is no longer connected to the south end of Kalihiwai Road since a tsunami took out the bridge years ago. Head toward the water on (W) Kalihiwai Road for .2 of a mile, then take the Y to the left, which will be 'Anini Road. In less than a mile, this road will follow the beach to the end at the 'Anini River. In the middle of this two-mile long beach (four miles from the start of 'Anini Road), you'll find the beach park with all facilities: shower, restrooms, covered picnic tables, small boat ramp and camping. Across the street (mauka) is the Kaua'i Polo Club.

As you leave Kalihiwai Road, the first stretch of 'Anini Road offers many lovely small pools, great for a quiet picnic or some wading. You may wish to enter the water here to have a gliding snorkel along the inshore reef, but will usually have to hike back on the street due to the slow, but relentless, current that heads west. You may want to tow along some flip-flops while you snorkel to save your feet from the hot road back to the car. When the current is strong, be extra careful as you cross any of the channels that head back to sea.

male spotted toby

Hurricane ʻIniki

Hurricanes don't brush Hawaiʻi often—only seven from 1950 to 1992, with just four actual hits. But the hurricane that roared over Kauaʻi on September 11, 1992, dubbed ʻIniki, was by far the biggest, a huge category four storm. It was unforgettable.

100 MPH winds with gusts as high as 143 MPH, waves of 20-30 feet, along with high tides pushed water in up to more than 20 feet above normal in some areas. Poʻipū was hit especially hard. Entire roofs were ripped off businesses, hotels and homes.

Before this quick-moving storm passed over, more than 14,000 homes in the south, west and north had been damaged or totally destroyed, 8 people were dead, and more than 100 injured. The winds were so severe that many trees lay uprooted, and those that stood still had been stripped of their leaves.

The rebuilding of Kauaʻi took years. Yet the Hawaiʻian land is quite resilient, and unless you were there before, you could vacation in Poʻipū today and not know that anything had happened.

Kalihiwai Bay

This broad sand beach in a protected bay can be reached from two sides, but the Kalihiwai River separates the two sections (see map, page 83). Kalihiwai Road used to be connected, but a tsunami many years ago washed out the bridge over the river.

For river access and camping, the west end is good with shade under the ironwoods along a river deep enough for good kayaking. Snorkelers and swimmers, however, will prefer to access Kalihiwai Bay from the sandy beach to the east of the river.

The eastern side of Kalihiwai Valley offers a relatively calm bay with wide sand beach, river to the left, and cliffs along the far right, where the bay is usually calmest.

When calm, this is an excellent swimming beach with some snorkeling along the cliffs. The middle is all sand. This is a popular family spot for picnics and boogie-boarding. Kayaking up the river is also very popular, although signs warn of leptospirosis danger, so be aware of this risk if boating or swimming in the fresh water. This is not a problem in the sea, only in fresh water.

Kalihiwai Bay is deep, well-protected and very pretty, although there are no public facilities in the area except portapotties in the east.

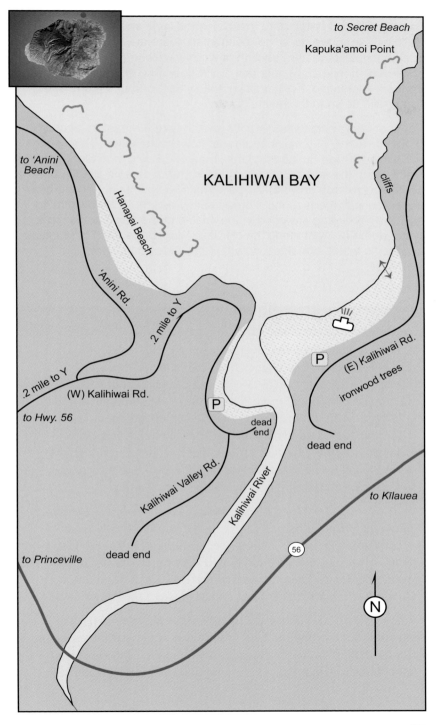

to Secret Beach

Kapuka'amoi Point

KALIHIWAI BAY

cliffs

to 'Anini
Beach

Hanapai Beach

'Anini Rd.

.2 mile to Y

.2 mile to Y

(W) Kalihiwai Rd.

to Hwy. 56

P

(E) Kalihiwai Rd.

ironwood trees

P

dead
end

dead end

Kalihiwai Valley Rd.

Kalihiwai River

to Kīlauea

dead end

56

to Princeville

N

GETTING THERE

Since the west and east sections of Kalihiwai Road are no longer connected, there are two ways to reach this beach. The western section of Kalihiwai Road (1.5 miles northwest at mile 25.5) gets you to the sand and the river, but not to the best snorkeling. For kayaking, follow this road to the end about half a mile down to the river.

For snorkeling and swimming, it's best to take the eastern section of Kalihiwai Rd. (1.5 miles southeast) toward the water. This section of Kalihiwai Road (just east of mile marker 24) will wind along the bluff toward the north. Stay left at the Y and eventually double back southwest to drop down to the bay. You'll find plenty of parking here under the ironwoods along a broad sandy beach. While swimming and body-boarding are good in the middle of the bay, snorkeling is better at the far right along the cliff (see map, page 89). Portapotties and picnic tables are also located on this side of the river.

Disposable Cameras

Cheap, widely available, even stocked on some excursions, and fun to use. Keep your expectations realistic and you won't end up disappointed, although don't expect to get pictures like you see in National Geographic. The professionals who get all those great shots use camera setups worth $10,000 and more. They also have assistants underwater to hold the lights and spare cameras. Their books start to look like bargains compared with trying to get these pictures by yourself! Check out the great selection of marine life books in Kaua'i bookstores.

Still, it's fun to try for that cute shot of your sweetie in a bikini, clowning with the fish. If you're lucky, you'll actually have identifiable fish in a few shots. The cameras won't focus closer than about four feet, so the fish will look much smaller than you remember them. These cameras work best when it's sunny with good visibility and the subject fish as close as the camera allows.

They do work OK above the water too, so make a great knock-around camera to haul around wet or dry without paranoia about theft, saltwater or damage. Try a picture of the beautiful mountains of Kaua'i as you float in the waters of Hanalei Bay.

scrawled filefish

Kauapea Beach (Secret Beach)

Secret Beach seems an odd name for a 3,000 foot-long sand beach that can be seen clearly from Princeville and extends from Kalihiwai Beach to Kīlauea Point. Is it secret because the path is so difficult? No, it's one of the easiest access paths that descend the bluffs in northern Kaua'i and it's only .2 mile long. The hike down through the ravine is relatively safe, entirely shady, and is well worth the effort even if big breakers typically make Kauapea too rough to snorkel or swim. While the path is not as dangerous as other north shore hikes, a heavy rain can make the muddy path more challenging. The "Secret" may have been finding the public trail down, which is not a problem with our map.

This is a gorgeous and uncrowded long stretch of caramel-colored sand with little shade. The hike will bring you down through a valley of tropical trees such as kiawe and breadfruit. The main public access path drops you down on the southern end of the sand, which is not usually the best place to snorkel. It is, however, a great place to walk on the beach, wade in the shallow protected ponds at the south end of the sand, and check out the cliffs with unusual basalt columns and caves with fresh water pools. A quarter-mile hike across smooth lava

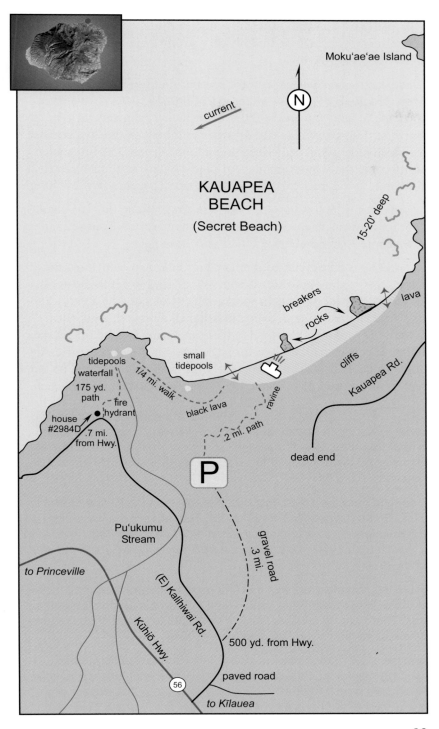

Moku'ae'ae Island

current

N

KAUAPEA
BEACH

(Secret Beach)

15-20' deep

breakers

rocks

lava

cliffs

Kauapea Rd.

tidepools
waterfall

small
tidepools

1/4 mi. walk

175 yd.
path

fire
hydrant

house
#2984D
.7 mi.
from Hwy.

black lava

ravine

.2 mi. path

dead end

P

Pu'ukumu
Stream

gravel road
.3 mi.

to Princeville

(E) Kalihiwai Rd.

Kūhiō Hwy.

500 yd. from Hwy.

56

paved road

to Kīlauea

will take you to a small waterfall with large tidepools big enough for snorkeling. When waves are low, very strong swimmers can snorkel to the left along the lava.

This beach sand changes with the seasons, but usually offers very protected pools of shallow water where little kids can have a great time, at the far south end of the beach where sand meets lava. In heavy surf, be extremely careful when climbing on the lava because a sudden large swell can sweep you into the ocean. The big winter storms take away huge amounts of sand, so this beach that stretches for a mile in summer can become three small beaches late in winter.

When calm, which is far more likely in the summer, this is a good spot for a swim. There are no facilities anywhere on Kauapea and few people—some wearing little or no clothing.

Snorkeling is best at the northern end of the beach, which requires a long, very sunny hike across one mile of sand to get to the north. While usually far too rough, snorkeling can be good on a very calm day. An experienced snorkeler can head out along the point and toward the Moku'ae'ae Island (a bird sanctuary) located off Kīlauea Point. This is never the place for beginners since waves can kick up quite suddenly. It's open ocean here with strong currents and no outer reef for protection. If in doubt, play it safe and just enjoy the beach.

GETTING THERE
There are numerous paths leading down to Kauapea Beach, but most are private. To get to the south end of Kauapea, take the eastern section of Kalihiwai Road that exits Highway 56 toward the lighthouse (just southeast of mile marker 24). See map, page 85.

If coming from the south, this is half a mile past the Kīlauea turnoff sign, .9 of a mile past mile marker 23. Turn toward the water here on (E) Kalihiwai Road, then take the first dirt road to the right, and follow it .3 mile to the end, where you can park and will easily see the start of the trail.

From the parking area, this trail first heads straight, then right, down into the ravine toward the sand. Parking is ample at the start of the trail. There are no facilities here or down at the beach. If you're going down for several hours, take water and hats.

Another VERY hidden trail is available for those heading to the western-most tidepools (see map, page 93). Park along (E) Kalihiwai Road near house #2984D. The nearly-invisible public access path is just east of the house, next to the yellow fire hydrant. This spot

94

is exactly .7 mile from Highway 56. The shady path between the fences drops down for 175 yards, then angles another 120 yards to a stream. You can easily cross the small stream and continue another 50 yards to the waterfall and tidepools.

While in the area, you might want to visit the Kīlauea Point Lighthouse at the end of Kīlauea Road. Although there is a parking fee, you'll enjoy the view from this northernmost point of the major Hawai'ian islands. Restrooms and a book store are located here at the end of the road. This is an important Wildlife Refuge, which includes the island of Moku'ae'ae just off the northern point. The whole Kīlauea area has a wonderful lush beauty, with dramatic rock formations and tropical greenery in every direction.

The Hawai'ian Public Libraries

There is a great resource available on all the islands—one of the best bargains in Hawai'i.

For just $25 with ID, any Hawai'ian library will issue you a library Card good for three years. This gives you full access to the rich and varied collections in the many local libraries. Believe us, if you take advantage of this, you'll be glad you did.

We make a stop at our local library soon after we arrive, checking out books on natural history, fish identification, Hawai'ian history and language, and much more. The "Hawai'iana" section in each library is a collection of books that include the above topics, and a good place to start.

You can check out a full range of VHS or DVD videos for a week for just $1 each (one of the few things that cost extra). Don't forget to try some music CDs or tapes, too. If you're interested, you can look over USGS topographic maps. Copy machines are available at ten cents per page.

All the libraries have internet terminals, and you can reserve an hour's session for free (though the sessions can be booked long in advance). You must hold a library Card to use the internet. Sometimes, you can pick up a quick ten minutes if the terminal is free between sessions. Pick up your email and browse the web. Or sit in comfortable chairs and read an assortment of local newspapers and magazines. Take a relaxing break in the hospitable libraries of Hawai'i.

East Area

The east coast of Kauaʻi offers pretty bays and beaches one after another along the whole northeastern coast. With extensive offshore reefs, there is plenty of snorkeling potential. However, nearly the entire east coast catches the prevailing northeast swell, making these lovely beaches dangerous most of the year. We don't recommend snorkeling or swimming when the usual surf is up and the rip currents are ripping. The long fringing reef, found offshore along most of the east coast is a popular fishing and limu (seaweed) collecting spot when the water is calm (only 3-4 weeks a year!)

When other east coast beaches are foaming with white water, Lydgate State Park near Kapaʻa is THE safest snorkeling site in Kauaʻi, having a man-made breakwater to stop the waves. Other beaches, like Anahola State Park, offer semi-protected corners where conditions can be quite calm depending on the exact swell direction.

Accommodations can be found at big hotels and condos near Highway 56 in Kapaʻa or at house rentals scattered through the towns of the east. Some are very secluded along quiet and uncrowded bays makai (toward the ocean) or mauka (toward the Anahola mountains). Some accommodations in Kapaʻa and Wailua front on small semi-protected segments of the coast.

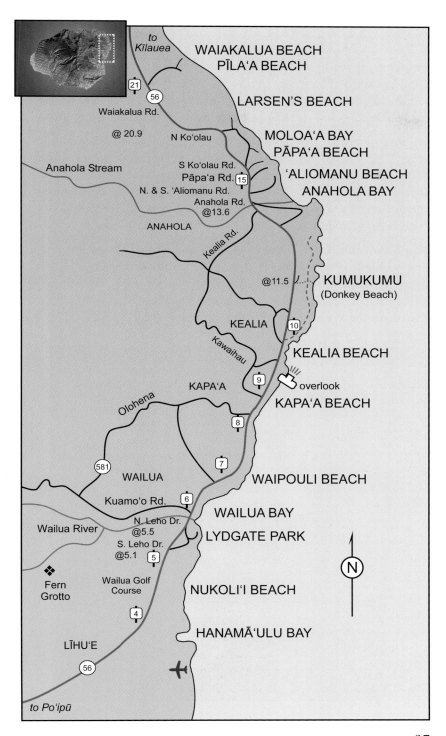

to
Kīlauea

WAIAKALUA BEACH
PĪLA'A BEACH

21
56
Waiakalua Rd.

LARSEN'S BEACH

@ 20.9

N Ko'olau

MOLOA'A BAY
PĀPA'A BEACH

Anahola Stream

S Ko'olau Rd.
Pāpa'a Rd. 15
N. & S. 'Aliomanu Rd.
Anahola Rd.
@13.6

'ALIOMANU BEACH
ANAHOLA BAY

ANAHOLA

Kealia Rd.

@11.5

KUMUKUMU
(Donkey Beach)

KEALIA

Kawaihau

10

KEALIA BEACH

KAPA'A

9   overlook

KAPA'A BEACH

Olohena

8

581

7

WAILUA

Kuamo'o Rd.   6

WAIPOULI BEACH

N. Leho Dr.
@5.5
S. Leho Dr.
@5.1   5

WAILUA BAY

LYDGATE PARK

Wailua River

❖
Fern
Grotto

Wailua Golf
Course

NUKOLI'I BEACH

N

4

LĪHU'E

HANAMĀ'ULU BAY

56

to Po'ipū

97

Along Highway 56 in Kapa'a, you'll find much of the shopping in Kaua'i, with two major markets. Golf courses, restaurants, and kayaking are readily available here and several of the rivers offer good kayaking. The rivers are lovely, but can bring lots of silty water to the eastern bays, making them murky when run-off is heavy. The reef offshore is also healthiest where there is less fresh water input.

We've listed the major bays and beaches, once again in clockwise order. There are plenty of beautiful spots, perfect if you want to get away from the crowds. Most of the best sites will require at least a short hike, if not a long and difficult one. If you are an experienced snorkeler and arrive on an unusually calm day, look over the conditions very carefully before deciding to enter the water.

You'll probably tire of hearing us write about the dangers, but tourists do drown themselves at these beaches — especially over-confident young men (according to the statistics). We want you to have a delightful AND safe snorkeling vacation in Kaua'i. The sites continue in our clockwise tour around Kaua'i.

orangeband surgeonfish

Kīlauea Bay (Quarry Beach)

Strong currents and undertow make this beach too dangerous for most snorkelers and the river can add to the danger. Kīlauea Bay faces northeast picking up prevailing swells from both directions, so it's popular with surfers. It's best to leave this one to locals who are more familiar with the changing conditions. We've been told that there is good snorkeling when conditions are calm, but we have not snorkeled this site. The reef follows the cliffs at the far north past the river and the rocks at the far south. In the middle, the sand drops off quickly providing the big waves for surfers.

This is a pretty site with lots of trees: ironwoods, hala and false kamani in the low dunes. Come for a picnic! Access is fairly easy with a short hike from the end of the bumpy dirt road.

GETTING THERE
From Highway 56, turn makai (toward the ocean) at mile 21.6 on Wailapa Road. Go half a mile, then turn left to "Kāhili Beach" on a winding gravel road, which dead ends at the south end of the bay. Hike toward the water for 200 yards and you'll find a long sand beach all the way to the river, picnic tables, plenty of shade, but no other facilities.

Wai'akalua Beach

While these two beaches are pretty and the hike isn't long, Wai'akalua is seldom a good snorkeling destination. The broad shallow reef catches eastern swells making it impossible to snorkel outside the reef most of the year. You'll be able to check out conditions here and at Pīla'a from the bluff where the hike begins.

Inside the reef, where it's calm, you'll find the water often too shallow for pleasant swimming or snorkeling. Stay away from any stream channels when swells are pounding the reef because all that water has to get out somewhere. You sure don't want to get swept out along with it.

Snorkeling is best around the point to the right toward Pīla'a, but you'll be lucky to find it calm enough. High tide is definitely best for adequate clearance here.

If you're just looking for a quiet spot for a picnic, then Wai'akalua might fill the bill. The trail down is especially steep, and slippery when wet, but not as dangerous as some. Of course, there are no facilities and no crowds here.

GETTING THERE

From Highway 56, you'll need to turn toward the ocean on North Wai'akalua Road (at mile 20.9). Head toward the ocean for .7 of a mile (see map, page 97), then turn left on a gravel road just before the end of the road. Continue on the gravel road lined with ironwoods to the end for .3 of a mile. You can park here and get a good view of the little beaches below.

The shady path is steep, slippery and about 175 yards to the bottom. At the base, you need to hike another 400 yards to the wide sand beach on your left. Hike along the sand (which can nearly disappear when surf is high in the winter.)

Mel Malinowski

bluefin trevally jack

101

Pīla'a Beach

Clockwise again, the next beach located south of Wai'akalua is Pīla'a. Pīla'a's two beaches catch the northeastern swell and are dangerous most days of the year. Requiring a long and difficult hike over some boulders from below or bushwhacking from the top assure the beaches are usually empty. The inner protected lagoon area is very shallow and very broad, so high tide is the best bet even on a good day. Stay well away from the channel when waves are high against the outer reef because all the water eventually sweeps out. Usually not worth the difficult hike unless you're looking for a very pretty and very secluded spot. As you can see in our picture, the sea does have quiet days here. If you find it like this and don't mind a very difficult hike, you'll enjoy the snorkel.

GETTING THERE   From Highway 56, turn toward the ocean on N. Wai'akalua Road at mile 20.9 (see map, page 103). Head toward the ocean for .7 of a mile, then turn left on a gravel road just before the end of the road. Continue on the gravel road to the end, then you will see Pīla'a's pretty beaches to the right as you look down from the bluff (see our picture above). This is a longer and more difficult hike than the one to the Wai'akalua beaches, but you can be sure to have a beach to yourselves.

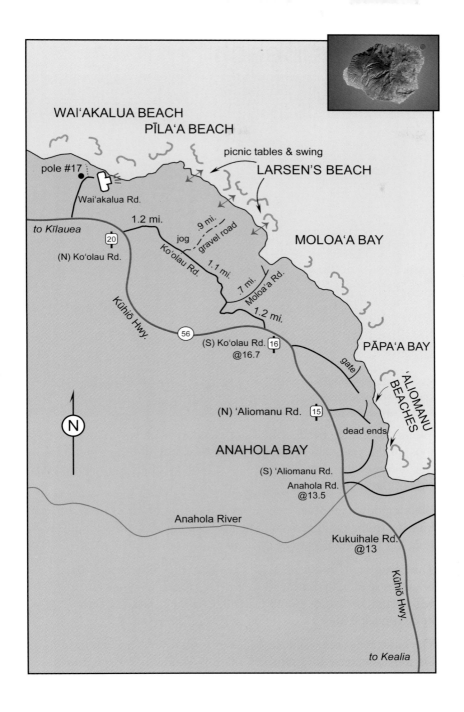

WAI'AKALUA BEACH
PĪLA'A BEACH

picnic tables & swing
LARSEN'S BEACH

pole #17

Wai'akalua Rd.

1.2 mi.

.9 mi.

jog

gravel road

MOLOA'A BAY

to Kīlauea

20

Ko'olau Rd.

(N) Ko'olau Rd.

1.1 mi.

.7 mi.

Moloa'a Rd.

1.2 mi.

Kūhiō Hwy.

56

(S) Ko'olau Rd. 16
@16.7

PĀPA'A BAY

gate

'ALIOMANU BEACHES

N

(N) 'Aliomanu Rd. 15

dead ends

ANAHOLA BAY

(S) 'Aliomanu Rd.
Anahola Rd.
@13.5

Kukuihale Rd.
@13

Anahola River

Kūhiō Hwy.

to Kealia

103

Larsen's Beach

While east-facing beaches in Kaua'i tend to catch waves and wind most of the year, you might get lucky here and find flat water. If so, this is one of the prettiest and longest of the secluded beaches on this side of the island.

Walking down involves only an easy five-minute stroll from the low hills down the gradual slope. The trail can get slippery after a heavy rain, but isn't dangerous or difficult.

The broad main trail leads to the center of the beach while other branches lead both north and south. This is a dry, somewhat windswept, area with plenty of sand. Pretty clusters of beach heliotrope and kiawe trees line the beach.

The outer reef protecting the beach gets waves most of the year, but the inner area provides safe, but shallow, snorkeling. High tide is definitely best if you like some clearance. Avoid the channels when there's any hint of currents sweeping out to sea. From the parking area, you may be able to see the rapids in the largest center channel. Stay well away from anything that looks like that! It's unlikely there will be anyone here to rescue you if you get caught in one of the rip currents. If in doubt, stay out of the water. These beaches exposed to the east swell are all for advanced snorkelers only at any time of the year because conditions can change suddenly. Take a long look and imagine what would happen to a snorkeler if a set of large waves suddenly crossed the reef. Winter and spring tend to be particularly dangerous on this side of Kaua'i, but the east can have huge waves and wicked currents at any time of the year. And with the east swells comes the prevailing east wind.

Still, Larsen's Beach is worth the pretty hike and offers parking under the ironwoods, picnicing under the kukui trees, and a nice stroll along the beach. You'll see some beach heliotrope thriving in this dry and windy location. This long, shallow reef is a popular limu (seaweed) harvesting site. The far north end of the beach has picnic tables and a rope swing, but there are no other facilities.

GETTING THERE

Ko'olau Road has a north and south exit from Highway 56. The north end is at mile marker 20 (see map, page 103) and is the closest. Heading toward the ocean from the northern end of Ko'olau Road, go exactly 1.2 miles, then take a gravel road to your left. There's an easily missed vertical pipe with "beach access" painted on it. Continue on this gravel road for .9 of a mile to the end, where you can park and look down on Larsen's beach. Hike 100 feet to the overlook, then 175 yards to a Y, where you take a right for another 120 yards to the water. The multiple trails here are overgrown, but passable.

To get to Larsen's from the south end of Ko'olau Road, go toward the ocean from Highway 56 at mile 16.7, then pass the road to Moloa'a Bay going a total of 2.3 miles from the highway till you come to the gravel road on your right with a vertical pipe that says "beach access." (the same one noted above). Head .9 of a mile to the end of the gravel road, where you can park under the ironwoods and catch a good view of the beach.

featherduster worm

Moloaʻa Bay

A gorgeous bay set down low in lush surroundings with an access road through a jungle setting, Moloaʻa is definitely worth a trip. There's little parking, but access is marked near the houses that line the beach. Park along the street as close as possible (see map, page 107), and walk as far as you must. While these eastern beaches in general can be rough, this one is a bit more protected by outer reef and the shape of the bay. It's also one of the prettiest, in a lush jungle setting surrounded by the hills on three sides. Please come with your best behavior and keep Moloaʻa spotlessly clean because we don't want residents of this quiet haven to build more fences.

The road stops at the houses near the middle of the bay where you will find beach access, but the water here is too rocky for swimming or snorkeling. Try walking along the sand to the picturesque far northern end (to your left) or to the far southern end for somewhat calmer water with safer entry. Watch the direction of the swells before choosing which way to hike. High tide is probably best if you prefer lots of clearance.

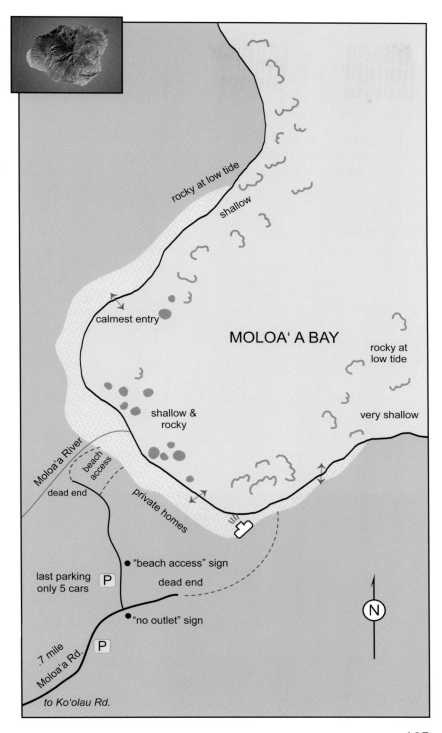

rocky at low tide

shallow

calmest entry

MOLOA'A BAY

rocky at low tide

shallow & rocky

very shallow

Moloa'a River

beach access

dead end

private homes

● "beach access" sign

dead end

last parking only 5 cars

P

● "no outlet" sign

.7 mile Moloa'a Rd.

P

to Ko'olau Rd.

N

There's plenty of sand along this quarter-mile long beach and space for secluded picnicking at either end of the beach. The bay's horseshoe shape helps stop the swells from most directions, but you still need to be cautious about currents sweeping out from the center. When calm enough, there is excellent snorkeling on both sides of the bay. But never, ever venture beyond the points.

Watch mainly for rip currents when waves are pounding the coral at the mouth of the bay. All that water has to somehow sweep back to sea and it usually does so from the center of the bay. No facilities are available here. Come early to find the limited parking located fairly close to the water.

GETTING THERE
From the south, take Highway 56 past Anahola, take the southern end of Ko'olau Road to the right (toward the ocean) at mile marker 16 (see map, page 107). Go 1.2 miles on Ko'olau Road, then turn right on Moloa'a Road. Follow Moloa'a for .7 of a mile and park where you find space (see map, page 107). There aren't many parking spaces near the houses, so be sure you don't block access to homes. You may need to double back to find parking along the road.

Continue walking from the end of the road to the far north. Depending on swell direction, you may want to park further south and walk to the south end of the bay. The area right in the middle is too shallow for good snorkeling and usually rougher.

From the north, take Highway 56 to mile marker 20 to find the northern end of Ko'olau Road. Turn toward the water here on Ko'olau and go 2.3 miles, then turn left on Moloa'a Road for another .7 of a mile.

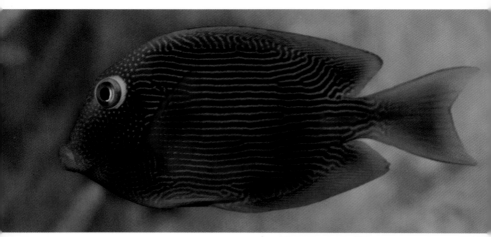

goldeye surgeonfish

Pāpaʻa Bay

Pāpaʻa Bay is completely surrounded by private property. A lush and gorgeous valley, but with no access beyond the guard station, it's hard to recommend for snorkeling. Should you manage to hike or boat in, the beach is very picturesque and supposedly has excellent swimming and snorkeling. It can have a strong current sweeping out from the center, especially in the winter.

One of Kauaʻi's scenic spots, Pāpaʻa Bay provided the setting for jungle and beach scenes in movies such as "Jurassic Park" and "6 Days and 7 Nights."

GETTING THERE
From Highway 56, just north of ʻAliomanu and south of mile marker 16, take Pāpaʻa Road toward the ocean (see map, page 107). This road ends at the bay, but has a guard posted to keep out the public. It is possible to hike in from further south, but it's a long, difficult hike. Consider other beautiful beaches nearby.

schooling eyestripe surgeonfish

'Aliomanu Beach

The 'Aliomanu beach area stretches from the northern corner of Anahola Bay to the southern edge of Pāpaʻa. Parts of 'Aliomanu are difficult to access, but this is a beautiful area and offers some swimming and snorkeling when seas aren't too rough. A large offshore reef catches much of the force of the east swell, although some of the higher surf will cross the reef.

The south end 'Aliomanu is along the north edge of Anahola Bay and attracts few beach-goers. The water near shore is studded with rocks and quite shallow, so swimming is tricky. Check our map (page 111) for a lovely spot to picnic and snorkel when calm. Always err on the side of caution. Since Anahola is a large bay, you'll want to drive here rather than hike from the far south. Be sure to stay well away from the river which may cause strong currents any time of year.

There is a long and wide fringing reef here, where collecting limu (seaweed) is very popular. 'Aliomanu provides the sought-after pink variety, so you may see people harvesting it out on the reef. This

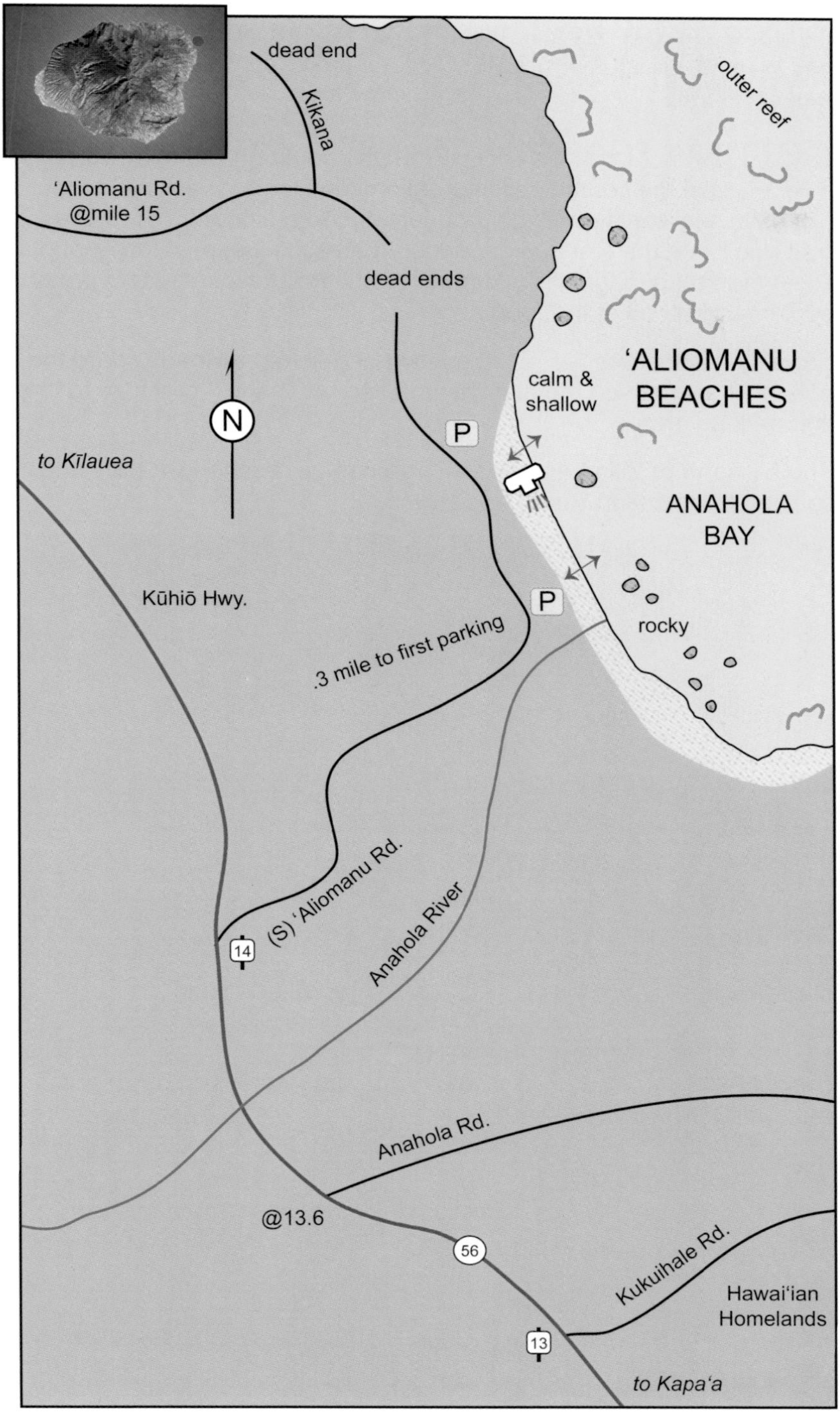

dead end

Kikana

'Aliomanu Rd.
@mile 15

dead ends

outer reef

calm &
shallow

'ALIOMANU
BEACHES

(N)

ANAHOLA
BAY

to Kīlauea

P

rocky

P

Kūhiō Hwy.

.3 mile to first parking

(S) 'Aliomanu Rd.

Anahola River

14

Anahola Rd.

@13.6

56

Kukuihale Rd.

13

Hawai'ian
Homelands

to Kapa'a

particular seaweed grows where the surf pounds, so don't try picking any yourself! High tide is best here for snorkeling within the vast inner reef area.

GETTING THERE
From the south on Highway 56 at mile 14, take the south section of 'Aliomanu Road toward the ocean. (The two segments no longer connect due to a tsunami.) At .3 of a mile you'll see the first parking under ironwoods just past the Anahola River (see map, page 111). Another .7 of a mile takes you to a pretty spot near the end of the road.

From the north, take the south section of 'Aliomanu Road toward the ocean when you see the highway marker 14. Drive .3 of a mile to the first parking area.

The far north of 'Aliomanu Beach area can be reached via the north section of 'Aliomanu Road.

Michel's goby on coral

If You Love the Reef

- Show respect for the reef creatures by causing them no harm.

- Avoid touching or standing on the coral, as touching kills it.

- Come as a respectful visitor rather than as a predator.

- Leave the many beautiful creatures you find there in peace so that others may enjoy them as you have.

- Allow the fish their usual diet rather than feeding them. Feeding them ultimately destroys their natural balance, and causes their numbers to decline. It also makes them more aggressive towards people, and can result in fish bites.

- Think of the creatures of the reef as fellow travelers in our life journey and then you may better grasp their true magnificence.

- Join our reef Easter egg hunt: try to find and dive for at least one piece of trash on every snorkel, and take it away with you. It sharpens your eye, and if enough folks do it, it will be hard to find any. Don't try to clean up the whole world. Just pick up one or two things every time you're out.

- Use sunscreen less, and cover-ups more. Sunscreen dissolves in the water, and is toxic to fish and coral. A lycra body suit or a wetsuit takes care of most of your body better anyway, and costs less than sunscreen in the long haul. Save your sun screen for your sensitive face, or wear a big hat.

Anahola State Park

Most of Anahola Bay is exposed to the eastern swells. Its angle does provide some protection, with the southern corner usually quite calm. That's where Anahola State Park is located, with restrooms, showers, parking, picnic tables, camping and a lifeguard station (but not necessarily a lifeguard). Local families like to camp comfortably in the lovely setting near facilities. Their "summer homes" are sometimes built with carport frames and can include color TV. Kids play in the shallow calm water and their parents fish from shore. This is a Hawai'ian Homelands area. Respect the locals priority, and they will treat you with aloha.

At the far southeastern corner, where the water is calmest, you can park under the ironwoods, relax on the heliotrope-lined sandy beach and enjoy a terrific view of "Sleeping Giant" in the beautiful Anahola Mountains.

The reef near shore is very shallow, so high tide is a must. Even then, some people will find it too shallow for comfort. This is a good place to wear a protective lycra suit if you have one.

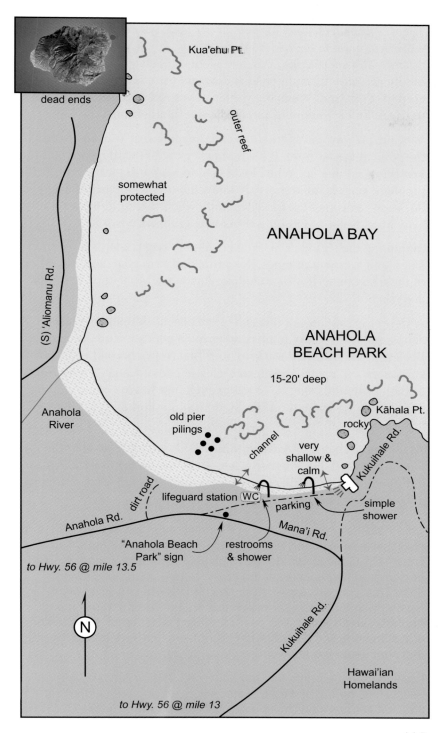

Kua'ehu Pt.

outer reef

dead ends

somewhat
protected

ANAHOLA BAY

(S) 'Aliomanu Rd.

ANAHOLA
BEACH PARK

15-20' deep

Anahola
River

old pier
pilings

Kāhala Pt.

rocky

channel

very
shallow &
calm

Kukuihale Rd.

dirt road

lifeguard station WC

parking

simple
shower

Anahola Rd.

Mana'i Rd.

"Anahola Beach
Park" sign

restrooms
& shower

to Hwy. 56 @ mile 13.5

Kukuihale Rd.

N

Hawai'ian
Homelands

to Hwy. 56 @ mile 13

There is a small channel located on our map, where you can snorkel without skimming the reef quite so closely. While snorkeling within the reef isn't spectacular, there are plenty of fish and the setting is excellent. Entry from the sand is easy and there is usually little or no current at this end. When big winter waves roll into the bay, it's wise to check for any outgoing currents in the small channel.

When calm, you can snorkel beyond the inner reef—even around the point at the far right. It's wise to check with the lifeguard before venturing out this far. While local visitors might suggest it's no problem, keep in mind that they know the ocean here better than you do. Venture beyond the inner reef only when you're sure it's entirely safe. Most of the bay is only about twenty feet deep.

Skimming the reef we saw needlefish, pink coral, interesting sea slugs, and a variety of tangs. We particularly enjoyed close-up views of the many butterflyfish including: lined, oval, four-spot, teardrop and raccoon.

A shower is available at this end of the beach, although it's just a simple pole that's easy to miss, so check the location on our map. Back near the lifeguard station you'll find restrooms and another shower. Bring a picnic lunch and relax in one of Kaua'i's magical settings with birds singing in the treetops. We always enjoy stopping here. Come for the natural beauty, and enjoy snorkeling if the tide is high enough.

At the opposite end of Anahola Bay you'll find more lovely beach with wider sand, but rougher water. There are no facilities at this end, but snorkeling is possible toward the point at the left. This is another good spot for a picnic.

GETTING THERE

From the south on Highway 56, turn right (toward the water) on Kukuihale Road at mile 13 (see map, page 115). Continue to the left when you come to a Y, then double back almost immediately at the next Y where you'll need to turn right. This road will lead you into the park where you'll find plenty of parking with facilities near the center. A sign will say "Welcome to Anahola Beach Park." The best snorkeling is at the far southeastern end of the beach. To park close, just drive to the very end of the road and park under the ironwoods.

Coming from the north, turn left on Anahola Road (at mile 13.5). Follow this road .7 of a mile to the beach, staying right at the first Y, then left at the second Y, where you'll see the welcome sign.

Discounts

Discounts are available for many excursions. If you're so in-clined, a little work and the right questions can save you a fair chunk of change. Begin by picking up one of the numerous free promotional magazines such as Kaua'i Gold. These are readily available at the airport, hotels and shops. They usually include special offers, coupons and other deals to attract customers.

Calling an excursion office and asking if there are any special offers can sometimes pay off, especially when tourism is slower. Summer and holidays the ships fill more quickly, but there is still plenty of competition on Kaua'i, so it's always worth a try.

Ships often charge less for children and nothing for toddlers. Each ship has its own definition of child and adult. Don't hesitate to ask about senior discounts, repeat customer discounts, and kama'āina rate (if you live in the islands and can prove it by showing your driver's license). Sometimes discounts are provided to AAA members.

For discounts ranging from 10-20%, try Activity Warehouse in Kapa'a. (808) 822-4000

If you have a browser, try: www.travelhawaii.com

It helps to have a flexible schedule and be able to go at the last minute.

For a free trip, sign up for a timeshare offer. You will have to sit through an hour or two of sales talk in exchange for your bargain trip. Do not underestimate their sales ability!

When you do book tickets ahead of time and charge them to your credit card, remember that when the ship goes out with or without you, you will be charged for the trip. The fine print usually requires you to cancel at least 24 hours ahead. You may wake up to weather that doesn't suit you only to find that the ship sailed anyway, and you will get to pay as agreed. Also, your destination isn't guaranteed. You might have your heart set on Lehua Island only to find the ship change to Kīpū Kai due to rough weather in the channel. This does not entitle you to cancel at no charge. Keep in mind they only make changes for true safety reasons, so go with the flow and trust your captain.

Kumukumu (Donkey Beach)

We've seen Kumukumu Beach recommended as a snorkeling and swimming destination, but the conditions are usually better for surfing than snorkeling. You'll have a long hot hike to get to the beach, then you will almost certainly encounter strong currents, big waves, and dangerous undertow with steeply-sloped sand. Needless to say, this is for experts only. No facilities closer than Kealia Beach. We recommend this area for hiking and biking, but bring water and hats and expect plenty of wind.

The name Donkey Beach comes from the days when donkeys (and humans) labored for the sugar plantation above the beach. You will see the remnants of an old landing along the trail south of the beach.

GETTING THERE   Heading north on Highway 56, take a right at mile 11.5 to the public parking near the highway (see map, page 119). At the south end of the parking lot, you'll find the public access path leading to the beach. At a quarter mile you'll cross the old cane road that follows the coast. Another 120 yards and you'll be

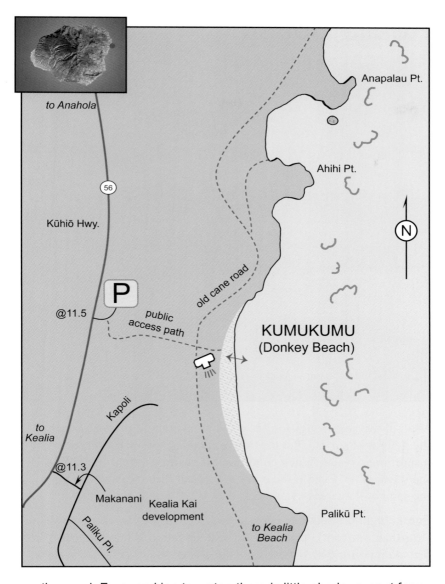

to Anahola

56

Kūhiō Hwy.

@11.5

P

public access path

old cane road

Anapalau Pt.

Ahihi Pt.

N

KUMUKUMU
(Donkey Beach)

Kapoli

to Kealia

@11.3

Makanani   Kealia Kai
                    development

Palikū Pl.

Kealia Kai
development

to Kealia
Beach

Palikū Pt.

on the sand. From parking to water, there is little shade, except for a beach heliotrope in the center of the lovely sandy beach.

The old cane road makes a pleasant hiking and biking trail heading south all the way to Kealia Beach and beyond, however, be prepared for sun and plenty of wind. There are other secluded pocket beaches in the area (depending on the season), but most are about twenty feet down fairly steep cliffs. Donkey Beach offers the easiest access to a beach.

119

Kealia Beach

Most of the year brings long rows of breakers to this broad beach to the delight of surfers, but the northern end is somewhat protected by a short breakwater. When conditions are calm enough, snorkel inside the breakwater. Even if the entry is safe, all these waves pounding the sand will decrease visibility.

Snorkeling the south end is possible ONLY if the waves are very low (less than one foot). A popular dive site is found about 200 feet from the south point, where there's a ledge under about 15 feet of water and another under about 25 feet. The water out here is often clear and it's just shallow enough for snorkeling. Look for the boulders encrusted with coral. You will probably see turtles, parrotfish, longnose butterflyfish and the pretty Picasso triggerfish. It's great snorkeling, but the catch is that it's calm enough for snorkelers only a few weeks of the year.

You'll definitely want to avoid the river toward the center of the beach. This beach is close to the highway, so you can easily check on conditions. The beach is somewhat bare with little shade, but quite beautiful. Kealia Beach is a nice place to walk, bike along the path, or explore tidepools. Parking is visible in several spots makai along the highway. Portapotties, picnic tables, more shade and a lifeguard are located at the north end, visible from a turnoff along Highway 56.

GETTING THERE

Between Kapaʻa and Kumukumu, you'll find Kealia Beach. To get there, go north on Highway 56 past Kapaʻa. After crossing the Moʻikeha Canal (see map, page 123), watch for turnouts along the makai (ocean) side of the highway near mile marker 10. You'll have a good view of the whole area before deciding whether it's safe to swim or snorkel. This is a great spot to see the height of the east swell that affects most of the beaches along the east.

lobster

Kapa'a Beach Park

This miles-long beach along the edge of Kapa'a (one of Kaua'i's 'big' cities) has easy access with restrooms and picnic tables in the center. You'll need to check out ocean conditions carefully and look for the spot that offers the best protection. Both ends of the beach are somewhat protected as is the center near the jetty. Choosing the best site will depend on the exact angle of the swells. And there are almost always swells from the northeast.

Kapa'a is a long beach requiring a drive to either end and has parking in several locations. You'll find a walkway along most of the beach. Clumps of ironwoods and coconut palms provide some needed shade. You'll see scattered picnic areas as well as a boat ramp into the canal near the southern end of the beach.

Snorkeling is good at the northern end of the beach when conditions are calm, but there are no facilities at this end. Park near the library and snorkel in the sandy-bottomed channel parallel to shore (see map, page 123). You might want to enter at the north end of the

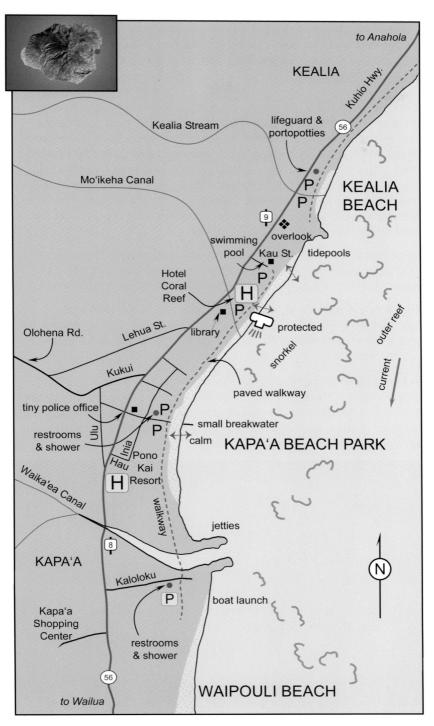

to Anahola

KEALIA

Kuhio Hwy.

56

Kealia Stream

lifeguard & portopotties

Mo'ikeha Canal

KEALIA BEACH

P
P

9

overlook

tidepools

swimming pool

Kau St.

Hotel Coral Reef

P

H

protected

snorkel

outer reef

Olohena Rd.

Lehua St.

library

current

Kukui

paved walkway

tiny police office

P

small breakwater

restrooms & shower

Ulu

P

calm

KAPA'A BEACH PARK

Inia

Hau

Pono Kai Resort

H

Waika'ea Canal

walkway

jetties

8

KAPA'A

Kaloloku

P

boat launch

Kapa'a Shopping Center

restrooms & shower

56

N

to Wailua

WAIPOULI BEACH

channel and drift slowly south. As usual in Kaua'i, stay well away from rivers and channels sweeping out to sea. Most of this inner reef area is quite shallow, so you may prefer high tide, although it isn't absolutely necessary.

GETTING THERE

Kapa'a Beach Park is found along the east of the city of Kapa'a. The center has the best parking, as well as restrooms and shower. To get to the center, turn toward the water at the tiny police station on the corner of Highway 56 (see map, page 123). You'll find restrooms and parking here as well as a walkway running in both directions along the beach. The small breakwater right in front offers some protection to its right. The outer reef here generally provides some protection from the worst of the eastern swells.

Kapa'a is a long beach with a paved walkway most of the way, so walk or drive to the calmest area before considering entering the water. Parking is available at several other spots along the beach.

To get to the boat ramp in the south, take Kaloloku Road from Highway 56 toward the water. You'll find plenty of parking, restrooms, and shower near the boat ramp. Since this park is so long, you may want to scout it out by car first.

Yet another entrance from Highway 56 is located at mile marker 9 further north. This one takes you to the Kapa'a public swimming pool and tennis courts near another somewhat calmer area. A very good snorkeling entry, but no facilities here. Definitely worth checking out when other nearby areas are too rough.

Mel Malinowski

milletseed butterflyfish

Waipouli Beach Park

Just south of Kapaʻa, you'll find small Waipouli Beach County Park, where seas are rough most of the year. It's a nice place to walk along the path connecting to Kapaʻa. Depending on the season, you may find little pockets of sand that are calmer.

GETTING THERE   Waipouli is just south of Kapaʻa, across the Waikaʻea Canal (see map, page 123). You can walk the beach from Kapaʻa or drive south to Waipouli Beach Park.

Wailua Beach

At the mouth of the Wailua River you'll find the beach with showers and restrooms. The shoreline trail stretches to the north end of Kapaʻa. This is a popular kayaking spot, but has heavy run-off from the river and typically catches some large eastern swells. It's definitely not a good swimming or snorkeling site most of the year. There are pockets of calm (especially in the south) when east swells aren't too high.

Sand gets removed and then returned, sometimes even blocking the river. Eventually the river will break through quite suddenly, which is fun to watch if you're there at the right time.

GETTING THERE   Located toward the ocean from the town of Wailua, this park is easy to find—located at mile marker 6 on Highway 56 near the Coconut Palms Resort.

Mel Malinowski

yellow tang

Lydgate Beach Park

Lydgate is Kauaʻi's calmest and safest year-round snorkeling beach. A man-made lava wall protects this beach from all the tradewind-driven swell. A delightful and easy snorkeling site, inspired by one in Sorrento, Italy, it's ideal for beginners and children. For you more advanced snorkelers and photographers, here's a chance to get very close to some beautiful fish that have learned to hang out with people. There's something here for everyone and it's an attractive full-service park as well. Plenty of parking, lifeguards, several restrooms and showers, expanses of grass and sand, covered picnic areas, and even a fish ID display. All this adds to the main attraction—the fish.

The central snorkeling pond ranges from threee to six feet deep and is large enough that it doesn't feel crowded (except on weekends.) Another pond just to the north offers an even shallower spot for toddlers to play safely. When and if they're done playing in the water, there's a children's park mauka (inland).

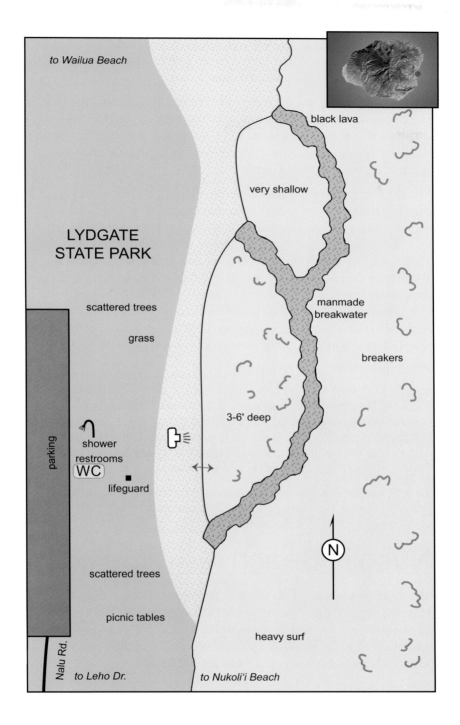

to Wailua Beach

black lava

very shallow

LYDGATE
STATE PARK

scattered trees

grass

manmade
breakwater

breakers

parking

shower

3-6' deep

restrooms
WC

lifeguard

N

scattered trees

picnic tables

heavy surf

Nalu Rd.

to Leho Dr.

to Nukoli'i Beach

127

For snorkeling at Lydgate, low tide brings clearer water. Most of the bottom is sand, so you don't have to sorry about skimming the coral. Just wander around the scattered coral heads.

It's annoying to see people here still feeding the fish, but signs are beginning to discourage this practice. You may notice that black surgeonfish and large chubs are more numerous at sites where people regularly feed the fish. These aggressive fish can easily crowd out some of the more colorful ones.

Middle of the day and weekends bring the crowds to Lydgate (making it more like a kiddie swimming pool), so you will prefer early mornings or late afternoon on weekdays. There could hardly be a better place to learn how to snorkel with absolutely no worries about swells or difficult entry. And the fish are large and exciting. We saw an excellent variety of butterflyfish, tangs, wrasses and even some large parrotfish. Big chubs swim about looking for handouts. Our favorites here are the scrawled filefish showing off their blue scribbled sides and the neon multi-colored yellowtail coris. We also saw a stripey, which is rarely seen at other sites.

GETTING THERE   From Līhu'e, heading north on Highway 56, turn right on Leho Drive toward the ocean (see map, page 127) just north of the Wailua Golf Course. This is .5 of a mile north of mile marker 5. Go .3 of a mile on Leho, then turn left on Nalu Road. From here it's just .2 of a mile to the park. You'll see the park entrance to the north and can easily find plenty of parking close to the water. You'll find all facilities in the center.

It's a bit longer, but you can also reach Lydgate from the southern end of Leho Drive by turning toward the ocean at mile 5.1. Then turn right on Nalu Road into the park.

Nukoli'i Beach (Wailua Golf Course)

Just south of Lydgate Park, you will find this two-mile long stretch of beach. According to the lifeguards at Lydgate, it's calm enough for snorkeling on as few as seven to ten days of the year (probably typical of the exposed eastern shore). Waves can really pound the beach, when rolling straight in from the northeast.

Snorkeling is good straight out from the golf course, but you have to find it almost flat. If you do, go for it! Sand varies with the season, so winter can be much rockier. Advanced snorkelers who can handle

128

a bit of swell should still be extra careful anywhere on the exposed east side of Kaua'i. Most of the exposed eastern shore of Kaua'i is for expert snorkelers only. Beginners should stay within the fully-protected Lydgate pool.

To find the best snorkeling spots at Nukoli'i, take the paved road through the golf course until it becomes a dirt road. Follow this road toward the sea to find some secluded little coves for the safest entry and exit. To find the same exit, it helps to mark your entrance point with a brightly colored bag.

The only facilities are located at the nearby Outrigger Hilton. In the ocean, found golf balls are free for surface divers.

GETTING THERE   Nukoli'i Beach is located just south of Lydgate Park. It stretches for about two miles with entrance either from the Outrigger Hilton or from the east side of the golf course. The rocky coast here offers several little coves where you can enter the water from a bit of sand only when the water is completely calm, which is rare.

raccoon butterflyfish

Līhuʻe Area

The Līhuʻe area near the airport is mostly hidden from the highway, but offers Kauaʻi's deepest and most sheltered bays—Hanamāʻulu and Nāwiliwili. These bays provide considerably calmer water than the beaches exposed to the full eastern swell. While surf can pick up here as well, there's often a chance of finding excellent conditions. These beaches can be shielded from prevailing east swells, winter north swells and summer south swells. They are worth checking when heavy south swell arrives along the Poʻipū area.

The Marriott is located on wide sandy Kalapakī Beach with plenty of water sports, great swimming, but poor snorkeling. Parking is the challenge here, so come early unless you're staying at the Marriott.

Other Līhuʻe beaches are often too murky for good snorkeling, but Ahukini Landing offers clear water (mostly about 30ʻ deep) with excellent snorkeling.

The Līhuʻe area offers a convenient central location near the airport. From here you can head either north or south, depending on the day's weather and surf conditions.

Hanamāʻulu Beach Park

The visibility here is very poor. While it improves as you swim out, it's still not a good snorkeling site. A very strong swimmer, however, could snorkel all the way to ʻAhukini Landing.

The beach park is a pretty site with a river and shallow area where children play in calm weather. There's shade under the ironwoods. Amenities include basic showers, restrooms, picnic tables and camping. It's a good place to shower after a snorkel at ʻAhukini Landing, but requires a longer drive than might appear since there is no access from Highway 51. This park was closed for two years due to pollution. Perhaps the large, calm bay doesn't have enough wave action to clean out this area near the river.

GETTING THERE   From the town of Hanamāʻulu on Highway 56, take Hanamāʻulu Road toward the ocean. There is a traffic light, but no sign so see our map, page 131. As this road angles under Highway 51, take the Y to the right on Hehi Road and follow to the park. Go left in the park to facilities at the northern end.

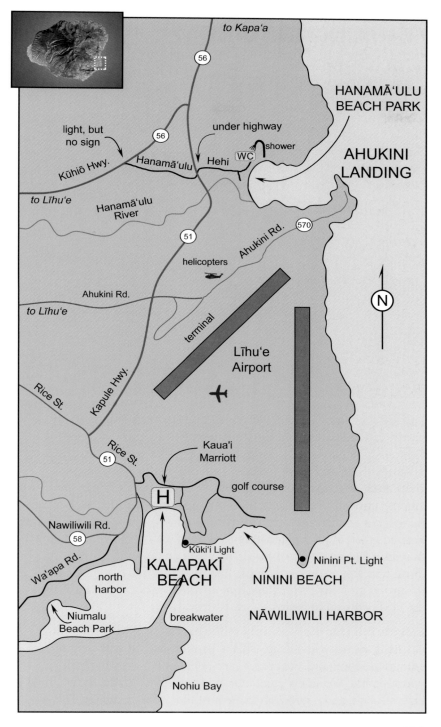

to Kapa'a

56

HANAMĀ'ULU
BEACH PARK

light, but
no sign

56

under highway

AHUKINI
LANDING

Kūhiō Hwy.

Hanamā'ulu

Hehi

WC

shower

to Līhu'e

Hanamā'ulu
River

51

570

helicopters

Ahukini Rd.

Ahukini Rd.

to Līhu'e

terminal

N

Līhu'e
Airport

Rice St.

Kapule Hwy.

Rice St.

51

Kaua'i
Marriott

golf course

H

Nawiliwili Rd.

58

Kūki'i Light

Ninini Pt. Light

Wa'apa Rd.

KALAPAKĪ
BEACH

NININI BEACH

north
harbor

Niumalu
Beach Park

breakwater

NĀWILIWILI HARBOR

Nohiu Bay

131

Ahukini Landing

Passing the airport, you can drive all the way on a progressively narrower road to Ahukini Landing, which is an excellent spot for fishing and a popular dive site. The deep water provides excellent visibility. Signs are now posted on the old pier that say "no snorkeling or scuba diving" (from the deteriorating old pier itself, we assume it means, but be careful if you go under the pier, as there are things you don't want to run into or have fall on your head). The area between the old pier and the breakwater is well-protected. Certainly this deep water site is not for first-time beginners and also not for those who fear sharks or pelagic fish. You'll also have to be careful to stay away from currents heading toward the ocean, so stay within the breakwater if in doubt.

Entry is from the rocks in front of the parking lot, where the water is fifteen to thirty feet deep. This is boulder habitat with a surprising amount of coral and a chance to see pelagic fish—even sharks if you're lucky. We saw a great barracuda, speckled butterflyfish, oval butterflyfish, and a good assortment of the usual creatures. This site

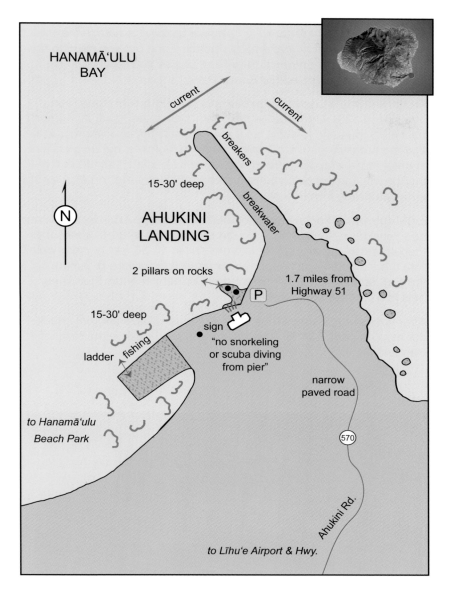

HANAMĀʻULU
BAY

current

current

breakers

15-30' deep

breakwater

AHUKINI
LANDING

N

2 pillars on rocks

1.7 miles from
Highway 51

P

15-30' deep

sign

"no snorkeling
or scuba diving
from pier"

ladder   fishing

narrow
paved road

to Hanamāʻulu
Beach Park

570

Ahukini Rd.

to Līhuʻe Airport & Hwy.

doesn't look too promising from the parking lot, but is definitely
worth a try. When calm, it's fine for beginners as long as they don't
feel a need to stand on solid ground. This is perhaps a good place to
prove that you can manage just fine without standing up.

Ahukini Landing can often remain very calm even when south swells
hit Poʻipū, so keep it in mind as an alternative when most of the
south shore is too rough.

GETTING THERE

Ahukini Landing is across the Hanamāʻulu Bay from Hanamāʻulu Beach Park, but you need to drive through the airport entrance to get to it unless you don't mind the long swim from Hanamāʻulu Beach Park.

From Highway 51, take the airport exit called Ahukini Road (see map, page 133). Continue on this road, staying left, past the airport, past UPS, past the heliport, as it meanders to the end where you'll find the breakwater. It's 1.7 miles from the highway, but an excellent snorkel that's well worth the drive. Ahukini Landing is at the end of the road by the old pier, where a prominent sign says "no snorkeling or scuba diving from the pier".

Enter the water from rocks in the center, where you can easily sit and don your gear. Snorkel either to the right along the breakwater or to the left under and around the old pier, all in 10-30 feet of clear water with the indigo blue of deeper water nearby. Be aware of fishers on the pier, so that you don't disturb them or get caught in their lines. This is a multiple use area.

After your swim, it's nice to shower at Hanamāʻulu Park, but check our map on page 131 for the only access road back in the town of Hanamāʻulu.

juvenile yellowtail coris

Ninini Beach

This small beach is tucked into the cliff area to the east of Kalapakī Beach. It catches eastern swells so is seldom calm, but offers good snorkeling along the cliff when that rare calm day arrives. You will need to either hike a short way down from the cliff or swim a long way from Kalapakī Beach.

GETTING THERE   Follow the directions to Kalapakī Beach (and see map, page 137), but continue on Hoʻolauleʻa Way past the hotel to the upper area, where there are several marked public parking areas located along the road. A variety of paths lead down the cliff. While none are long, they all require caution.

It's probably easier to swim from the east end of Kalapakī Beach and avoid the hike over rocks, but it's a long swim and only for experienced snorkelers.

adult yellowtail coris

Kalapakī Beach (Nāwiliwili Park)

This large protected cove within Nāwiliwili Bay sits in front of the Kaua'i Marriott. It's a lovely setting with a river at the western corner and sheer cliffs bordering the eastern end of the bay. Parking and all facilities are available at the public park near the river, but snorkelers are better off at the eastern end, where limited public access is provided by the hotel. Since parking spots here fill early, come by 9 a.m. to use this end of the beach. Otherwise you'll have to wade through the shallow river and hike the full quarter-mile length of Kalapakī Beach.

In spite of the protection within Nāwiliwili Bay, swells can and do pick up—especially in the winter. Usually though, you'll find Kalapakī much calmer than most of the eastern coast. Kalapakī Beach is popular for swimming, surfing, and kayaking.

On calm days, park in the hotel spots designated for the public (see map, page 137) and snorkel the eastern end of the beach far out along the cliffs toward Kūki'i Point. If it's very calm, try going around the point, but always stop if you encounter any current or big swells. Although Kalapakī offers excellent swimming, we were disappointed by the snorkeling. You'll see nothing but sand in the center and

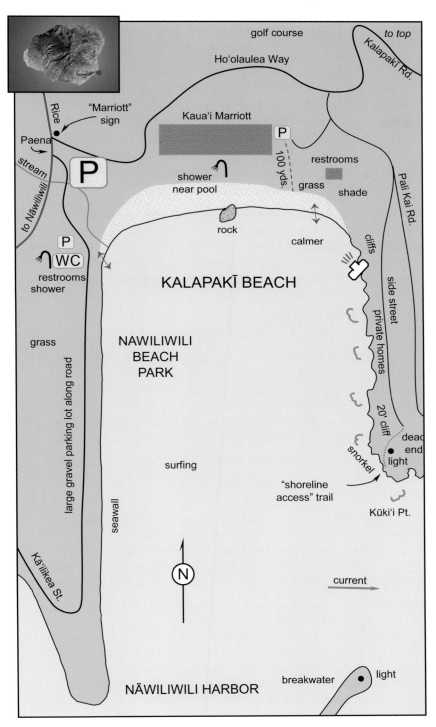

golf course

to top

Kalapakī Rd.

Hoʻolaulea Way

Rice

"Marriott" sign

Paena

stream

to Nāwiliwili

Kauaʻi Marriott

P

100 yds.

restrooms

grass

shade

Pali Kai Rd.

P

shower near pool

rock

calmer

cliffs

side street

P

WC

restrooms shower

KALAPAKĪ BEACH

private homes

grass

NAWILIWILI BEACH PARK

20' cliff

dead end

light

snorkel

"shoreline access" trail

Kūkiʻi Pt.

large gravel parking lot along road

surfing

seawall

N

current

Kāʻilikea St.

breakwater

light

NĀWILIWILI HARBOR

few fish along the rocks in the protected bay. The sand slopes very slowly, providing safe swimming in five to ten feet of water.

Kalapakī is a pretty spot where you can lounge on grass or sand under the palm trees with restrooms inside the unlikely-looking building to your left. Hotel showers are near the pool, while the public shower at this end has disappeared. For a quick trip up to the bluff, take the elevator within the building where the restrooms are located. It will take you to the upper area lagoon, but it's still a long, hot hike to the edge of the bluff, then a scramble over rocks if you want to snorkel Ninini Beach.

Better yet, drive up the road to find several spots up the hill toward the east where you can have a great view of Nāwiliwili Bay. Some parking areas have paths down to the water, but none of the paths are easy since most of this corner is very rocky. It's better to enjoy the view or a short hike than try to climb over the rocks to snorkel near the entrance of Nāwiliwili Bay, Kaua'i's main port. As we write, this upper area looks somewhat abandoned—especially the shopping center near the point. This may change eventually.

GETTING THERE

Kalapakī Beach can be reached from the west or east. The popular public beach with facilities is located at the western end of the bay where the river empties into the bay. From the north, on Highway 50, take Rice Street (Highway 51) toward the water (see map, page 137). Watch carefully and turn toward the water on Paena into the fair-sized public parking area.

From the south, take Highway 56 north, then head right on either Nāwiliwili St. or Rice St. (Highway 51) toward the water. Paena will be on your left.

Or, to avoid the crowds, arrive from the south on Kā'ilikea Street where you will see signs to Nāwiliwili County Park (see map, page 115). The park here offers plenty of shade, sand, grass, showers, restrooms, and picnic tables. Parking is usually available along the road by the seawall—since people tend to come and go frequently.

For the best snorkeling access, take Rice Street in Līhu'e (Highway 51) toward the water. Then turn left toward the Kaua'i Marriott on Ho'olaule'a Way. Drive east past the hotel entrance until you see the public access sign to the right. You will drop down to the Marriott's eastern parking lot with about ten designated spaces for the public in the southeastern corner. When these fill, people do park along the road. The hotel seems to allow this as long as cars aren't blocking the road to the parking area.

Follow the broad flagstone path about 100 yards south to the lovely eastern end of Kalapakī Beach, where you'll find a bit of snorkeling along the cliffs at the left, but few fish or coral. Kalapakī is better for swimming or other water sports than snorkeling. Pick your spot: sand or grass, shade or sun. Restrooms are available in the building to the left (east) of the sand. A shower is hidden back near the hotel's pool.

Although seldom calm enough for snorkeling, the area beyond the eastern cliffs can be reached by driving to the upper lagoon area, where a number of steep paths lead down to the water. You'll find designated parking spaces up here too—even though the lots are nearly empty. This is worth a drive just for the view of Nāwiliwili Bay. Snorkeling is better here, but only for experienced swimmers since you'll find exposure to open ocean.

To walk from the eastern end of Kalapakī Beach, simply walk into the building with the restrooms and take the elevator to the upper level. You'll have about a half-mile long hike to the beach, but it's a lovely view of the harbor and sea from the top of the hill.

Niumalu Beach Park

This beach further inside Nāwiliwili Bay is fine for camping and kayaking, but there is too much fresh water run-off with its poor visibility, so you won't find good snorkeling here.

GETTING THERE   From Kalapakī Beach, head southwest on Waʻapa Road or Niumalu Road. You'll find the park just to the west of the main harbor (see map, page 137).

Mel Malinowski

squirrelfish

Poʻipū Area

Poʻipū is the most popular vacation spot in Kauaʻi. People go for the sun (often less than twenty inches of rain a year), warm weather, a large assortment of accommodations, golf, and plenty of restaurants. Large hotels offer luxurious rooms and amenities of the total destination. Inexpensive condos can be found, some even have an excellent ocean view. Houses for rent are also common here, so you'll have plenty of choices.

While the majority of folks hang out at their resort pool or beach, there are some excellent snorkeling sites too. Some of the beaches are protected by outer reef, and some are protected from southern swell by their angle and offshore reef. When south swell picks up (most often in the summer), you do have some choices here in case a given beach is too rough.

In many ways, safe snorkeling is easier to find than good swimming because most of the beaches have somewhat shallow reef. The big hotel beaches (such as the Sheraton) usually have good swimming,

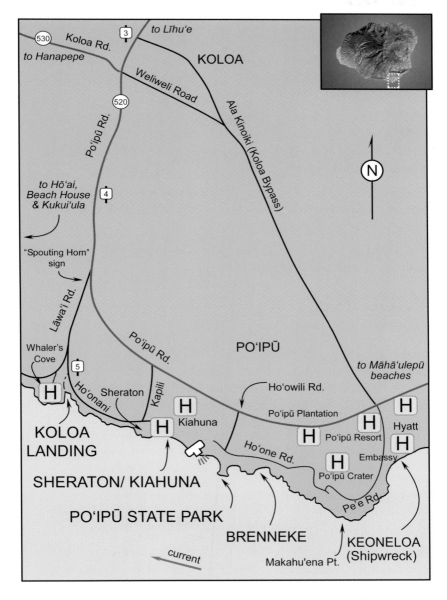

but less well-known snorkeling sites (such as Kōloa Landing and Beach House) will often be calmer.

For excursions, the town of Hanapepe is only a half-hour drive west, where you'll find boats leaving from Port Allen.

Of special interest in the south are the Māhā'ulepū beaches (our first four sites). All are along the coast between Po'ipū and the lovely

Hāʻupa mountain range. Roads may change in the future, but for now, entry is through dirt roads across what used to be cane fields. The sugar cane is gone since it's no longer profitable, so various experimental fields are now in use. Poʻipū itself may eventually encroach on this lovely area.

The further east you head from Poʻipū through the Māhāʻulepū area, the more wind-swept the beaches are. Watch the form of the trees — if most of the trees are bent over at a 45 degree angle, it's probably a windy spot!

The south has plenty to offer most of the year with popular public beaches, wide sand hotel beaches, secluded snorkeling sites, and unexpectedly good snorkeling at little bays.

We'll start at the northeastern end when describing these sites, continuing with our clockwise listing.

Kīpū Kai

Public access to the Kīpū Kai beaches is, for the time being, prohibited and the single road across the Hāʻupa Mountains is private. There are actually four beaches at privately-owned Kīpū Kai. Snorkeling is excellent if you ever have a chance to give it a try. We look forward to the day when it will be open to the public.

GETTING THERE   The lovely Kīpū Kai area is too remote (and surrounded by mountains) for an easy hike. Perhaps in the future, excursions and kayaks will again be able to enjoy this beautiful setting.

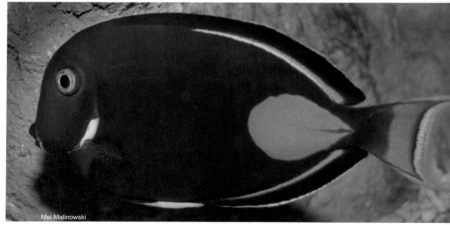

Mel Malinowski

Achilles tang

Hāʻula Beach

This windswept beach southwest of Kīpū Kai can be reached by a 15 minute hike from the end of the gravel road (see map, page 145). While it's a dramatic setting, the waves are much too rough here for either safe swimming or snorkeling most of the year. The bay is tucked into the surrounding hills with sand dunes lining the back. While Hāʻula rarely provides safe water sports, it does offer excellent seclusion. All beaches in the area are beyond a gate and guard station (open 7:30 a.m. till 7 p.m.)

GETTING THERE   Take Poʻipū Road past the Hyatt and continue driving as the road becomes gravel. The worst of the pot holes are here, but the road gets better further along. Pass the golf course and stables on your right. You'll be headed directly toward Hāʻupa Mountain. At the main intersection of gravel roads, where you see the power lines intersect, turn toward the ocean. This road is located 1.8 miles past the Hyatt. Turn right, then pass the quarry and the guard shack. Continue .7 of a mile (keeping right at the Y) until you see a parking area near the beach. One dirt road to the left is blocked, but another is available.

Turn left here and continue driving east on the rough dirt road for .3 of a mile until you see Kawailoa Beach (see map, page 145), then continue driving east on the dirt road along the coast for another .3 of a mile. When you get to the end (for non-4WD vehicles anyway), park and hike in the same direction over wind-swept terrain toward the next beach. It's pretty in a stark way, but not a snorkeling destination under typical conditions.

Kawailoa Beach

Our favorite beach in this area, Kawailoa Beach can be reached from the dirt road after it passes Gillin's Beach. It's a beautiful spot with easy access from the dirt road. The beach itself is small and picturesque—an excellent spot for a quiet picnic or some fishing. Snorkeling is best if you hike along the sand to the right to the inner protected area along a curved reef close to the shore.

While you can hike a path over the sand dunes to get here from Gillin's Beach, it's closer and easier to park in the shade along the edge of Kawailoa Bay—providing the rough road isn't too muddy.

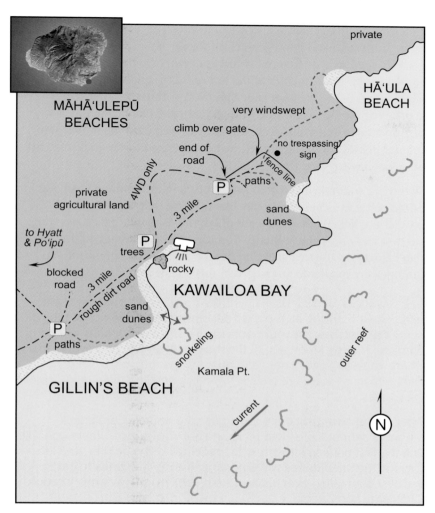

MĀHĀʻULEPŪ
BEACHES

private

HĀʻULA
BEACH

very windswept

climb over gate

end of
road

no trespassing
sign

private
agricultural land

4WD only

fence line

paths

P

.3 mile

sand
dunes

to Hyatt
& Poʻipū

P

trees

blocked
road

.3 mile

rough dirt road

rocky

KAWAILOA BAY

sand
dunes

P

paths

snorkeling

Kamala Pt.

outer reef

GILLIN'S BEACH

current

N

trumpetfish

145

Enter the sheltered area marked on our map (page 145) for an easy entry from sand and good protection for an inner reef near the shore. Usually there is a drift here toward your right (to the southwest), so you might want to enter at the left (eastern) end of the reef and slowly drift to the western end. Stay well within the outer reef, snorkeling on the ocean side of the inner reef. On a calm day, beginners can enjoy this spot, but the stronger currents in this area require good swimming ability, just in case the current picks up. By all means, wear your fins.

When big south swells roll in (more often in the summer), stay out of the water at isolated beaches like this one that have minimal protection. When conditions are good, this is a great place to swim, snorkel and enjoy the solitude. You can still see damage to the reef caused by Hurricane 'Iniki, but the fish are still plentiful. No facilities are available anywhere in this isolated area.

GETTING THERE

Take Po'ipū Road past the Hyatt and continue driving as the road becomes gravel, then pass the golf course and stables on your right. You'll be headed directly toward dramatic Hā'upa Mountain. At the main intersection of gravel roads, where you see power lines, turn right toward the ocean. This intersection is located at exactly 1.8 miles past the main entrance of the Hyatt.

After a right turn, past the quarry, pass the empty guard shack (keeping right at the Y) and drive another .7 of a mile, where you will find the first parking lot (see map, page 121). The path to your left through the sand dunes will wind up and over the dunes to get to the best snorkeling eventually. It's a nice hike up the dunes through Christmas berry trees.

Alternatively, when you come to the parking area, take the second dirt road to the left and it will reach Kawailoa Beach, where you can park just steps from the sand. This next bay is just .3 of a mile east of the parking for Gillin's Beach. We prefer this spot because it's pretty, shady and a great place to picnic. To get to the best snorkeling, simply hike back to the right along the sand. You'll be able to see the inner reef that curves out from the sand. Enter the water at the left (east) end of the inner reef since the current heads to the right. When waves pick up a bit, an outer reef offers some protection from south swells, but the offshore current is still usually fairly strong even when surf is low.

146

Gillin's Beach

Gillin's Beach is located near the first parking area, where you arrive at the Māhā'ulepū beaches. Just a short hike from the parking area, you'll emerge from the kiawe trees to find a beautiful long almost-white sand beach. Snorkeling here is good if south swell is very low, but can be quite hazardous when it picks up. Waves and currents can catch you and there won't be anyone to see it happen.

This is a lovely spot to walk the long beach and picnic on the sand under the ironwoods. Listen for the pleasant bird songs and flashes of colorful birds. No facilities here and few people.

This same parking lot has a path to the left that will eventually lead to the safest snorkeling spot (between Gillin's and Kawailoa). There's plenty of reef along Gillin's Beach, but it's shallow, with rocky and difficult access. Begin at the easiest access, then experienced snorkelers can explore further out.

GETTING THERE

From Po'ipū, head toward the Hyatt, passing the hotel, then the golf course, then the stables—all on your right. The road is now gravel, but wide and heads directly toward Hā'upa Mountain rising almost straight up 2,297 feet.

At exactly 1.8 miles past the Hyatt, you'll come to an intersection with power poles (not telephone poles as they're usually described). Take a right turn here, pass the quarry and empty guard shack and head .7 of a mile (keeping right at the Y) to the sand dunes parking area.

This first parking area (see map, page 145) has two roads leading in either direction as well as two paths closer to the middle of the parking circle. The path (not the road) to the right leads about 75 yards through the kiawe trees to Gillin's Beach, where you'll find a beautiful long beach lined with ironwoods and trees full of birds. You might be able to hike a mile on sand in either direction and not see a single person.

Keoneloa Beach (Shipwreck)

This long, pretty beach in front of the Hyatt is nice for a stroll and tanning. It tends to be rougher than others in the Po'ipū area, so isn't the best bet for either snorkeling or swimming. If you happen to catch it on a very calm day, snorkel along the cliffs at the left end of the beach. Leave jumping off the cliffs to the locals. There is some public parking at the eastern end of the beach.

GETTING THERE   Take Po'ipū Road east past the Hyatt. Then take Ainako Road toward the beach. You'll find a parking lot with public access, showers, and restrooms, but not the safest swimming or snorkeling, especially when south swells from distant storms arrive in the summer.

Brennecke Beach

Brennecke, although next door to Po'ipū Beach Park, is definitely NOT a snorkeling or swimming beach. You might want to pause and watch the body-surfing. Brennecke seems to catch all the waves from the south and sand drops off quickly forming a strong undertow. If you want a risk much, much bigger than sharks, body-surf here and try not to break your neck when a quick-breaking wave dumps you on your head in the sand. Still, many folks body-surf here and have a great time. Be careful if you're new to the sport!

GETTING THERE   Brennecke is the first beach to the east of the Po'ipū Beaches (see map, page 151), located along Ho'ōne Road just to the east of Po'ipū Beach Park. Parking is not allowed on the road near Brennecke, but you'll find two large parking lots across the street from Po'ipū Beach Park. You might want to snorkel at the beach park, then duck over to watch the kids body-surfing at Brennecke Beach.

Poʻipū Beach Park

Located in the center of the Poʻipū area, this popular beach is better for snorkeling than swimming. The distinctive spit of sand connecting the shore to the rocky area offshore is one of the few examples in Hawaiʻi of a tombolo (see page 151). This division creates two separate back-to-back beaches. Snorkel to the right (west) anywhere within the area protected by offshore reefs. The beach to the left is equally good when swells are similar. Pick the day's calmest side.

While the beach itself is smooth sand, the underwater area is strewn with large boulders making you vulnerable if sudden waves are high enough to cross the offshore reefs. Take a good look at conditions before you enter the water and inquire at the lifeguard station if you have any doubts. Just because lots of people swim here, doesn't mean it's entirely safe for either swimming or snorkeling. As long as waves stop at the outer reef, it's all very easy, but sudden waves can and do cross the reef. This happens when waves roll in from storms in the Southern Pacific.

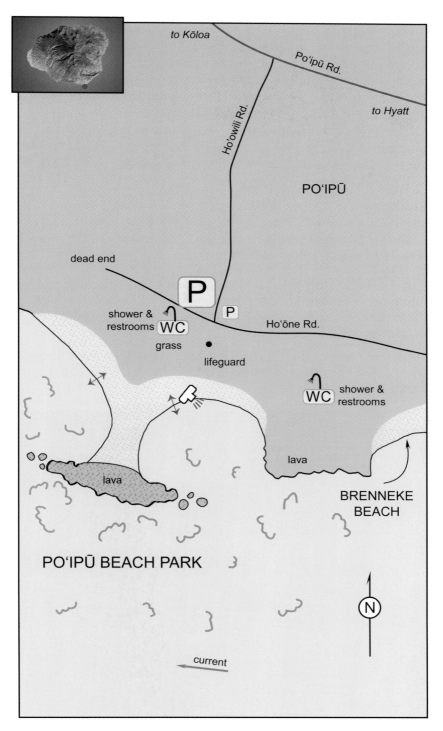

to Kōloa

Poʻipū Rd.

to Hyatt

Hoʻowili Rd.

PO'IPŪ

dead end

P

P

shower &
restrooms WC

grass

Hoʻōne Rd.

lifeguard

WC shower &
restrooms

lava

BRENNEKE
BEACH

PO'IPŪ BEACH PARK

N

current

151

Snorkeling here is not as good as it was before Hurricane 'Iniki and you'll see some of the damage to the reef. At least the junk (like sewing machines) has been removed by now. Still, it's a lovely beach with all facilities and you're certain to see some fish. Showers, restrooms, covered picnic areas and lifeguard are available. It's a nice place to hang out on sand or grass with some shade under scattered palms. Although popular, there's usually ample parking available in the large dirt lots mauka (toward the mountains). People come and go frequently, so wait a bit if necessary and you'll find a spot to park.

Snorkeling is in three to fifteen foot deep water where you can wander around amid the boulder habitat while being careful to stay within the protected area. When the sea is very calm, you can snorkel around the outside of the tombolo.

GETTING THERE
Po'ipū Beach Park is located next to the corner of Ho'ōne Road and Ho'owili Road on the beach side of the town of Po'ipū. Park in one of the gravel lots on the corner (see map, page 157).

In case you're confused: the beach in front of the Sheraton is sometimes called Po'ipū Beach, while Po'ipū Beach Park is the one with a tombolo in the center.

adult rockmover wrasse

Tombolo

Poʻipū Beach Park has an unusual and interesting sand formation know as a "tombolo". Tombolos form when an offshore rock or small island bends the waves around it so that they meet and deposit sand in a spit that eventually extends from the island to the shore. Perhaps the most famous tombolo is that connecting Mont St. Michel to mainland France. It is submerged at high tide.

Tombolos are occasionally washed away by periods of strong wave action, but eventually re-establish themselves.

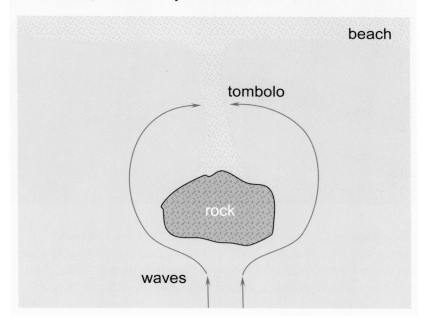

juvenile rockmover wrasse

Kiahuna/Sheraton Beach

This long beautiful curve of sand stretches from the Kiahuna Plantation to the Sheraton Hotel. It's also called Po'ipū Beach, which can easily be confused with nearby Po'ipū Beach Park. Parking and public access are provided, but the best spots are difficult to find. Check our map (page 155) to find the more convenient spots close to the best snorkeling otherwise you may have to hike the length of the beach, or more. And, of course, come early.

For snorkeling, enter from the sand at the eastern end of the Sheraton and snorkel in the most protected area. Watch the waves closely because waves are somewhat, but not entirely, caught by the offshore reef. Entry is usually easy from the sandy beach, although there are some rocks to avoid even in a low swell. Of course, snorkelers can see them more easily than swimmers. Since the beach slope is sometimes moderately steep, be alert for a surprisingly strong undertow close to the edge. Not enough to be a problem unless you fall over onto a sharp rock.

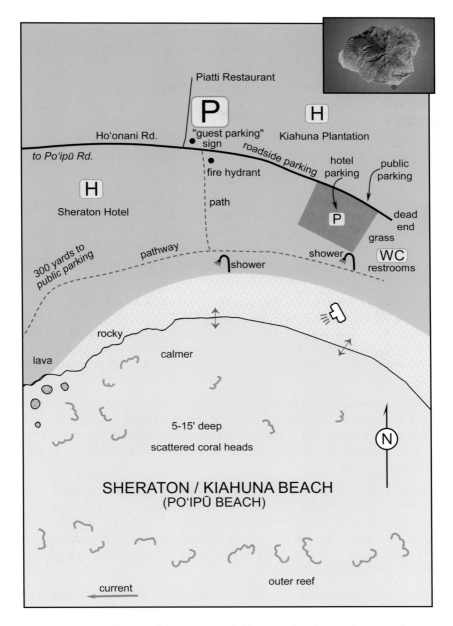

Swimming is also good here, especially on calm days when south swells aren't bad. Out a bit you'll see mostly rubble with some small lobe and encrusting coral heads in five to ten-foot depth. There's plenty of room to explore, but don't wander into surfing territory beyond the outer reef.

This reef was damaged by Hurricane 'Iniki, but you'll still find plenty of interesting fish, such as tangs, boxfish, needlefish, colorful wrasses and large cornetfish.

Kiahuna Beach is well worth a trip and a nice spot to enjoy the beach with showers and restrooms handy. Pretty as it is, the waves can still pick up when storms arrive from the South Pacific (mostly in the summer), so check the swells carefully before entering the water. As at most of these beaches, mornings tend to be calmer than afternoons when winds may pick up.

GETTING THERE

This long sand beach is bordered by the Sheraton Hotel and the Kiahuna Plantation. Public parking is available in several spots (see map, page 155), but we prefer the small lot at the east end of the Sheraton. This spot has good access to sand, showers, restrooms, grass, and offers easy entry for snorkeling or swimming.

From Kōloa, take Po'ipū Road toward the ocean. At the first Y hold to the right (which is Lāwa'i Road) and take the second Y to the left, which is Ho'onani Road). Follow Ho'onani along the beach nearly to the end. You'll pass the Sheraton Hotel makai (on your right, toward the ocean). Public parking is available in at least three locations (see map, page 155).

Midday, when parking gets tight, you might have better luck parking just to the west of the Sheraton. It's a longer hike (about 300 yards) along a concrete path that traverses the entire front of the hotel. There are twenty one parking spaces here with a shower at the far west end of the lot.

Toward the middle of the Sheraton, there's more hidden "guest parking" in the shaded lot mauka of the Sheraton. The sign says "guest parking for Piatti Restaurant, Kiahuna Plantation, and day beach access only." It's directly across Ho'onani Road from the fire hydrant. From here you'll find a path through the Sheraton grounds to the west end of the beach.

Beyond the east end of the Sheraton, you'll find the last and best parking lot with beach access parking. This spot gets you within twenty yards of the beach, where you can enter for good snorkeling or swimming. Restrooms are located across the grass to the east and a public shower is found toward the beach. This parking lot fills very early.

Doctor My Eyes

If you are swimming along snorkeling peacefully and your vision suddenly loses focus, don't be too quick to panic and call for a doctor. While you may have had a stroke or the water may be oily, there is a much more likely cause: You've just entered into an outdoor demonstration of the refractive qualities of mixtures of clear liquids of different densities. Is that perfectly clear?

Near the edge of some protected bays, clear spring water oozes smoothly out into the saltwater. As it is lighter than the mineral-laden saltwater, it tends to float in a layer near the surface for a time. When you swim into it, you'll often notice a sudden drop in the water temperature. The fresh spring water can be downright chilly.

Now, clear spring water is easy to see through, as is clear saltwater. If you mix them thoroughly, you have dilute saltwater, still clear. But when the two float side by side, the light going through them is bent and re-bent as it passes between them, and this blurs your vision. It's much like the blurring produced when hot, lighter air rises off black pavement, and produces wavy vision and mirage.

These lenses of clear water drift about, and often disappear as quickly as they appeared. Swimming away from the source of the spring water usually solves the problem. Clear at last?

sleeping parrotfish

157

Kōloa Landing

Popular with kayakers and divers, this site doesn't look like much and has no facilities other than the boat ramp and a dozen parking spaces. It does offer surprisingly calm water with good snorkeling. Consider coming here when south swells kick up during the summer.

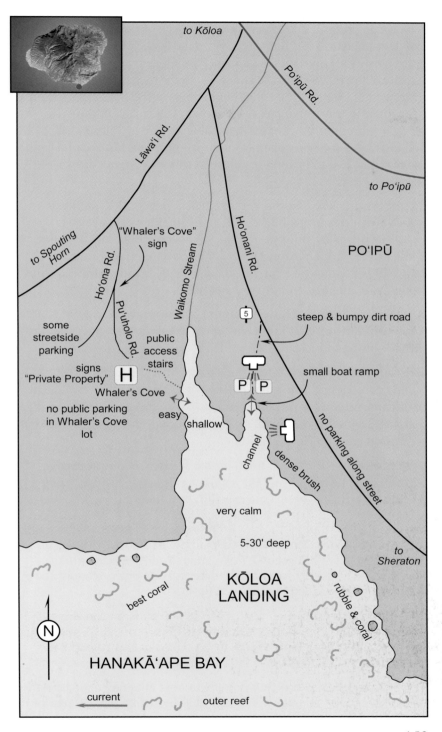

to Kōloa

Po'ipū Rd.

to Po'ipū

Lāwa'i Rd.

to Spouting Horn

"Whaler's Cove" sign

Ho'ona Rd.

Pu'uholo Rd.

Waikomo Stream

Ho'onani Rd.

PO'IPŪ

some streetside parking

public access stairs

signs "Private Property"

H

5

steep & bumpy dirt road

Whaler's Cove

P   P

small boat ramp

no public parking in Whaler's Cove lot

easy   shallow

channel

dense brush

no parking along street

very calm

5-30' deep

to Sheraton

best coral

KŌLOA LANDING

rubble & coral

N

HANAKĀ'APE BAY

current   outer reef

159

Kōloa Landing is hidden from view, so check our map (page 159) or you will likely miss it. Entry is easy on the boat ramp with its gentle slope. Just walk right into the channel taking care not to fall on the usually slippery ramp. In the water watch for rocks even if there's only a small swell as you enter, but there's decent clearance right in the center (at least three feet). Snorkel anywhere—left, right and straight in front of the ramp. There's lots to see very close to shore and the bay is well-protected from the bigger waves offshore. Depth ranges from five to twenty feet close to shore, dropping deeper as you head out to sea.

We enjoyed an evening snorkel here when most of the south had big swells and poor visibility. At Kōloa Landing we saw turtles in the deeper areas, huge parrotfish, schools of tangs so thick you couldn't see through them, Moorish idols, trumpetfish, and pairs of butterflyfish—teardrop, longnose, blue-striped, and multiband. And we had the little bay entirely to ourselves.

Another day we saw about a thousand bluestripe snappers and a large scrawled filefish. What fun! Don't go here for the ambiance, but just for the marine life.

The short, steep dirt road that drops down to Kōloa Landing is bumpy enough that you might hesitate to drive down in a rental car or anytime after a heavy rain. If you're adventurous and good at dodging deep ruts, you can drive right on down and park. No parking is allowed back on Hoʻonani Road.

If intimidated by the rough road, try the Whaler's Cove access, which entails a swim across the small river which is usually murky and shallow. Swim slowly and carefully to avoid running into rocks.

GETTING THERE

From the town of Kōloa, head south toward the water on Poʻipū Road. Hold right at the first Y (Lāwaʻi Road), then left at the second Y (Hoʻonani Road). Watch carefully and you'll immediately see a rough dirt road that drops steeply down to Kōloa Landing (see map, page 159).

The road is rutted, so you might prefer to find parking elsewhere and walk down. Kōloa Landing is located right at mile marker 5 and looks more like a driveway than a road. It has space below for about a dozen cars, but no facilities, sand, or shade.

Enter Kōloa Landing straight through the boat channel in the center, where it's usually very calm. Walk carefully because the wet part of the ramp can be treacherously slippery with algae.

160

Hanakāʻape Bay (Whaler's Cove)

The Whaler's Cove lot no longer provides public parking spaces, although some parking is available along nearby streets. From inside the lot (to the left) you will see beach access signs leading to a short hike down stairs. You'll have to enter from the river here in order to snorkel out into Hanakāʻape Bay, so will appreciate high tide. It's also a bit rockier here and murky, so our preference is to enter from the Kōloa Landing boat ramp. Either way you will find a good snorkeling destination in usually calm Hanakāʻape Bay.

GETTING THERE   From the town of Kōloa, take Poʻipū Road toward the beach. At the first Y hold right (Lāwaʻi Road), at the second Y hold right (still Lāwaʻi Road), and at the third Y, hold left (Hoʻōne Road)—see map, page 159. At the fourth Y, hold left on Puʻuholo Road. Immediately turn left into the Whaler's Cove, where you must park along the street. The public access path is located at the far left of their lot (see map, page 159). The steps will drop you down at the west side of the river. High tide is better here if you want the easiest entry. Most people would prefer the ease and comfort of the boat ramp, especially if they don't wear booties. The entry at Whaler's Cove is rocky, with no sand or any facilities.

hawkfish

Hō'ai Bay (Prince Kūhiō)

Although the Prince Kūhiō Park across the street from this bay is not open to the general public, you can park along the street to snorkel in this small, mostly-protected bay. This isn't a great swimming spot because of all the rocks and the shallowness near shore, but the snorkeling is excellent. Study the bay for a bit and you'll find a narrow sandy entry channel near the center. It's only about a foot wide, but gives you a chance to walk in to a larger sand-bottomed area where you can put on fins and adjust your mask at your leisure. Then it's easy to snorkel over the reef, which is ten to twenty feet deep within the bay.

Depending on the season, you may find a small sandy beach in the right-hand corner Although we've seen snorkelers enter the water on the right, the center seems safer and more dependable to us. At low tide, the entry is quite shallow, but there's plenty of clearance just a few yards away and in most of the bay. Take care even if swells are low since it's easy to fall on the rocks as you enter or exit with a small swell.

162

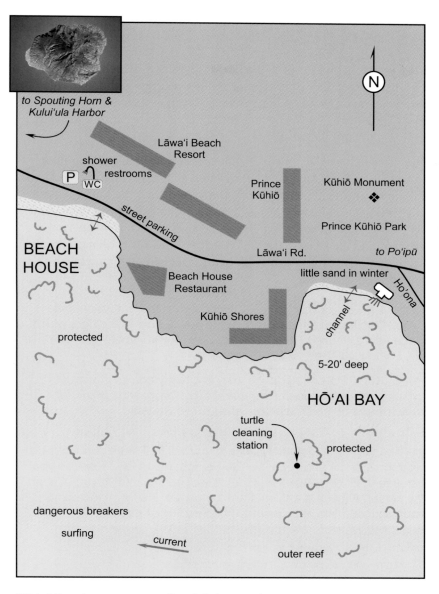

to Spouting Horn &
Kuluiʻula Harbor

shower
P ↑ restrooms
WC

Lāwaʻi Beach
Resort

street parking

Prince
Kūhiō

BEACH
HOUSE

Beach House
Restaurant

Kūhiō Shores

protected

Lāwaʻi Rd.

N

Kūhiō Monument
❖

Prince Kūhiō Park

to Poʻipū

little sand in winter

Hōʻona

channel

5-20' deep

HŌʻAI BAY

turtle
cleaning
station

protected

dangerous breakers

surfing

current

outer reef

Hōʻai Bay is a great spot for sighting turtles. We've marked the spot
on our map where turtles congregate straight out from the eastern
edge of Kūhiō Shores. Last time we were there we saw at least ten of
them from one spot—some resting on the bottom, others swimming
around, eyeing us curiously.

Coral isn't too exciting here, but we found a great variety of fish:
lots of orangeband surgeonfish and yellow tangs, schools of Moorish

idols, parrotfish, pairs of butterflyfish (threadfin, fourspot, ornate), and a spotted eagle ray hanging out not far from the turtles.

Don't get tempted to snorkel around the point to Beach House because it's rougher off the point and not deep enough to provide good clearance should a bigger wave sweep in. Leave that area to the ever-present surfers. Watch the current here too because it tends to pull you toward the west.

We've seen lots of people have unnecessary trouble walking in or out of Hōʻai Bay. Any site like this with a narrow entry and rocks to fall on can be a challenge if done the wrong way. Walking in or out wearing fins can be hazardous because a small swell can throw you on a rock. Simply keep fins in hand, walk slowly out to the sandy spot beyond the swell, then don your fins and you're all set. Exit the same way, so that you don't risk being knocked on the rocks by an unexpected wave.

GETTING THERE

Heading south from Kōloa, take Poʻipū Road toward the ocean. At the first Y, hold to the right which is marked "Spouting Horn." This is Lāwaʻi Road, where you will drive directly to Hōʻai Bay (see map, page 141).

Prince Kūhiō Park (map, page 164) is directly across the street (mauka), but is not open for general use. The condos at the far western end of the beach are called Kūhiō Shores.

Park along the road next to Hōʻai Bay or further up Lāwaʻi Road near the Beach House restaurant, where you will find more parking, plus restrooms and a shower. Hōʻai Bay is right next to the road, so you can see the little patches of sand as well as the small channel near the center. Access is easiest from the center. Parking these days fills early as these two beaches have become more popular.

Hawaiʻian dascyllus (damselfish)

Beach House (Lāwaʻi Beach)

This bay in front of the Beach House restaurant on the way to Spouting Horn has excellent snorkeling with easy entry from the sand when calm. There's a parking lot with shower and restrooms right across the street as well as more parking along Lāwaʻi Road. The beach itself is sometimes called Lāwaʻi (although there is a private Lāwaʻi Beach further along to the west) and also often confused with Hōʻai Bay a short walk to the other side of the Beach House restaurant.

This is a small bay so come in the early morning or late afternoon if you want to avoid the crowds. Surfers will be catching waves further out, but the inner area is somewhat protected and often relatively calm when south swells hit in the summer. You'll have to watch out for a drift to the right that is stronger when those surfers are getting good waves. Take care on entry because even a small swell can knock you onto a sharp rock. It's best to put fins on after you've crossed to a deeper area with more clearance. Remove fins early when returning to shore, just as the sand begins.

Beach House Beach has an excellent variety of fairly tame fish and some scattered coral patches, all quite near shore in about 5-15 feet of water. The water isn't terrifically clear when south swells arrive, but you can get quite close to the fish here, so get a good look anyway. We saw a 3-foot crocodile needlefish with impressive teeth being cleaned by a cleaner wrasse. We saw schools of flattailed needlefish, many large cornetfish, and even a rare monk seal!

Mel Malinowski

endangered Hawai'ian monk seal

Monk Seals

When visiting Kaua'i, you may be lucky enough to see a very rare sight, the handsome Hawai'ian monk seal. Fewer than 1500 remain, making them one of the most endangered seals in the world. It is illegal to kill, capture or harass them. They often crawl up on the edge of the beach for evaporative cooling.

Most of the monk seals live in the Northwest Hawai'ian islands, the remote remains of the island chain to the NW of Kaua'i. They feed on lobsters, octopus, eels other than moray or conger, flatfish and other small reef fish, and small invertebrates. They can dive to 500 feet, and remain underwater as much as 20 minutes. Adults weigh 300-600 lbs. and grow to about 7 feet long.

The creatures here can vary quite a bit day to day, so can range from disappointing to fantastic. Since this isn't one of Kaua'i's most picturesque sites, you might come on a poor day and wonder why you bothered. All we can say is that it CAN be great. Put in your hours with that snorkel and you'll be amazed what you find. Check out our picture of the startled snorkelers here just feet from shore who find themselves face to face with a monk seal. Having snorkeled nose-to-nose with a monk seal, we know how they feel! The monk seals can be quite curious, but let them do the approaching. They have been know to bite overly familiar tourists.

If you want to see turtles and don't find them here, just walk on down to Hō'ai Bay on the other side of the restaurant and Kūhiō Shores. You'll find them at the spot marked on our map.

These two beaches offer similar conditions, but the entry at Beach House is easier for a beginner since there's more sand, especially at the end of the winter when Hō'ai has practically none. Both beaches usually have a slow current that tends to pull you to the right (west), so snorkelers need to look up now and then to avoid trouble. By all means, stay out of the surfing area.

GETTING THERE   Heading south from the town of Kōloa, take Po'ipū Road toward the ocean (map, page 141). At the first Y, hold right toward Spouting Horn. This is Lāwa'i Road. You'll pass small Hō'ai Bay, then Kūhiō Shores and Prince Kūhiō condos. Just past the Beach House restaurant, you'll see the beach (see map, page 164). Some parking, restrooms and shower are all located directly across Lāwa'i Road. There is also parking along the side of Lāwa'i Road.

monk seal meets surprised snorkelers

Kukui'ula Bay

Just to the east of Spouting Horn, you'll find the quiet Kukui'ula small boat harbor. It's well-protected by the breakwater, with a bay that offers unusually calm conditions for swimming or snorkeling in five to fifteen feet of water. The breakwater at the southeastern end (to the left) provides good snorkeling with good visibility, especially near the end. Facilities include restrooms, showers, picnic tables and plenty of convenient parking.

Entry is very easy from the center of the little sandy beach, although the water is somewhat murky near the sand. It gradually improves and is quite good by the middle near the breakwater. We saw pretty pearl wrasses, several turtles, and a good variety of the usual reef fish. Check this site when south swells in summer make other south-facing beaches too rough.

Caution: stay very alert for small boats coming around the breakwater, especially when there are large swells, when they would have more trouble spotting you. We prefer to snorkel either close to the breakwater or zip across the bay away from any boat traffic.

GETTING THERE   Head west on Lāwaʻi Road passing Hōʻai Bay and Beach House. You will see the harbor off to your left (makai) before you get to Spouting Horn (see map, page 141). From Lāwaʻi Road, take either Alania Road or Amio Road toward the water at the east end of the bay. This will bring you to the parking and all facilities. Enter the water from the sandy beach (easiest) or directly from the breakwater. Snorkel near the breakwater or across the bay in order to avoid boat traffic. Venture beyond the breakwater only when seas are very calm. In choppy water be extra careful to watch for boats since they may have trouble seeing you over the swells.

Lāwaʻi Bay

This gorgeous bay probably offers great snorkeling, but has no public access at the moment. It can be seen from above in the Allerton Gardens tour. Several other beautiful bays along this section of Kauaʻi's south coast also lack access due to the private-property guarded cane fields. We hope that this changes some day.

Southwest Area

On the other Hawaiʻian islands the most reliable snorkeling and sunniest weather is usually found on the southwest coast, but Kauaʻi is different because of its full exposure to the Pacific. Southwestern Kauaʻi does get more sun than the rest of the island and has abundant sand, but also has plenty of surf, with heavy currents offshore. This surfing territory seldom offers safe swimming or snorkeling. Salt Pond Beach is an exception where you will find a natural lava breakwater that usually provides very safe and interesting snorkeling.

Most of the southwestern beaches are pretty and dramatic with few tourists, so they offer excellent places to hike and escape the rain. On the rare day when you find calm water the swimming and snorkeling can be quite good.

Port Allen (only a half hour from Poʻipū) offers many excellent snorkeling excursions. We highly recommend a trip to Lehua Island near Niʻihau. There is a charming and delicious Thai restaurant in the quiet local shopping center near the excursion offices.

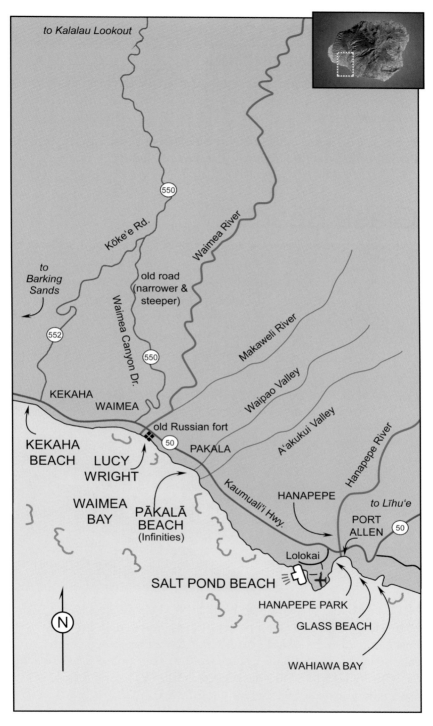

to Kalalau Lookout

550

Kōke'e Rd.

Waimea River

to
Barking
Sands

552

old road
(narrower &
steeper)

Waimea Canyon Dr.

550

Makaweli River

Waipao Valley

A'akukui Valley

Hanapepe River

KEKAHA

WAIMEA

old Russian fort

50

PAKALA

Kaumuali'i Hwy.

HANAPEPE

to Līhu'e

KEKAHA
BEACH

LUCY
WRIGHT

WAIMEA
BAY

PĀKALĀ
BEACH
(Infinities)

WAIMEA BAY

HANAPEPE

PORT
ALLEN

50

Lolokai

SALT POND BEACH

HANAPEPE PARK

GLASS BEACH

N

WAHIAWA BAY

Wahiawa Bay (Ahulua Bay)

This sandy beach, with cliffs along both sides, offers protection from both winds and currents. Heavy runoff from the river can make the water murky, but snorkeling can be good when there's little rain up in inland mountains.

Public access is unavailable at this time, but dirt roads do run across the fields makai of the highway just west of Numila.

Glass Beach

Not a snorkeling or swimming destination. This little beach gets its name from some well-worn pieces of glass in the sand. It's a tiny beach immediately east of Port Allen. After a little beach combing, follow the dirt road a short distance to the east (beyond Glass Beach) for a lovely hike that hugs the rugged shore. Well worth a stop, especially toward sunset, but only for the hike.

male bird wrasse

female bird wrasse

GETTING THERE   From Līhuʻe, take Highway 50 west to Hanapepe. Then head for Port Allen on Waialo Road before the Hanapepe River. This little beach is immediately to the east of the port behind the prominent fuel tanks (along Akaʻula Road). After a stop at Glass Beach (or skipping it), continue about a quarter mile along this dirt road east to the end at the old cemetery, where you will see the start of a trail along the dramatic shoreline. This is a lovely place to watch waves, with waterspouts, natural bridges and a peek at the next bay.

Hanapepe Beach Park

Located near the mouth of the Hanapepe River, this beach gets too much silt to offer good snorkeling. It does have restrooms, showers, and parking. It is also reputed to have plenty of hammerhead sharks.

GETTING THERE   From Līhuʻe, as you approach Hanapepe on Highway 50, this park is located at the western corner of Hanapepe Bay (see map, page 171). This is near Kauaʻi's largest harbor on this side of the island. Excursions depart from Port Allen Harbor to the Nā Pali Coast and Lehua Island near Niʻihau.

Salt Pond Beach Park

An outer reef as well as a natural lava breakwater usually fully protect this sand beach except for the gap in the center. Salt Pond is an excellent choice when swells kick in from the south. Stick close to either end if in doubt about the swells or current. The water at either end is very shallow and usually calm enough for toddlers.

You'll find plenty of parking, showers, restrooms, large covered picnic areas, grass, sand and shade. The wide beach is mostly sandy with some rocks, and the water is just deep enough for swimming. Snorkeling is excellent with a variety of large fish near shore. With the easy entry and one to ten foot depth, it's like a salt water swimming pool. Because of the gap in the lava at the center of the beach, there can be a current, so you should still use fins and watch children carefully, especially if you see any sign of swells crossing the breakwater.

Snorkeling is excellent at either end, but our favorite is a very shallow nearly enclosed corner near the far southeastern end of the

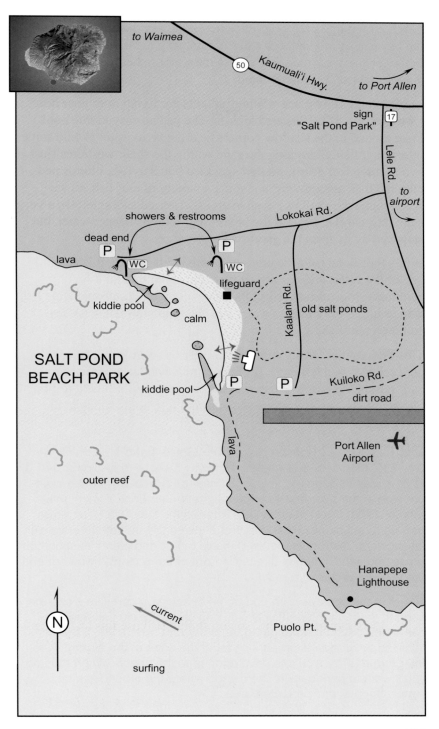

to Waimea

50 Kaumuali'i Hwy.

to Port Allen

sign "Salt Pond Park"

17

Lele Rd.

to airport

Lokokai Rd.

showers & restrooms

dead end

lava

P

WC

P

WC

lifeguard

kiddie pool

calm

Kaalani Rd.

old salt ponds

SALT POND
BEACH PARK

kiddie pool

lava

P

P

Kuiloko Rd.

dirt road

Port Allen
Airport

outer reef

Hanapepe
Lighthouse

N

current

Puolo Pt.

surfing

175

beach. You might prefer high tide here. The dirt road at this end of the bay can be muddy after a heavy rain, so you might want to park in the lot and walk the short way to the water rather than risk getting your rental car stuck in the mud.

You're in the right place when ultralights are flying over your head. Don't be put off by this area looking like just an easy kiddie pool. Poke around in the shallow corners near the breakwater to find some interesting fish. Skimming the sand within the shallowest area (just two to three feet deep), we saw speckled butterflyfish, bluestriped butterflyfish, ambon toby, and quite a variety of reef fish, so we recommend the shallows even to an experienced snorkeler. On a very calm day, snorkel beyond the breakwater into the deeper water, but stay well away from the great surfing territory.

While Salt Pond isn't the prettiest beach in all Kaua'i, it is certainly one of the safest and easiest, so we highly recommend it for beginners. More advanced snorkelers will enjoy occasional large fish wandering in from deeper water and close-up views of some less common reef fish.

This is a popular family spot used mostly by local folks, especially on weekends and holidays. If time permits, hop back in the car and snorkel the northwestern end too, because you're likely to find different fish. You'll find the showers and restrooms handy at the north end.

GETTING THERE
From Līhu'e, head west on Highway 530, then continue west on Highway 50 (see maps, page 171 & 175). Cross through the town of Hanapepe (Port Allen) to the western side of the river and watch for signs to Salt Pond Park at mile marker 17. At the sign, take Lele Road to the left. After .3 of a mile, turn right on Lokokai Road for .6 of a mile until you see the park with its showers, restrooms, covered picnic tables and plenty of space on grass and sand. Snorkel directly in front of the park (the western end of the semi-enclosed beach).

To get to the southeastern end of the beach, you can hike along the sand to your left. Alternatively, you can cross the old salt pond by car on the paved road to get to the other end, where you'll find no facilities other than a dirt parking lot at the edge of the airport. When the ground is dry, you can drive right up to the beach. When muddy, you'll want to park back in the dirt lot, where the ground is a bit firmer. Snorkel any protected area.

176

Pākalā Beach (Infinities)

Pākalā is a very popular surfing area, dubbed Infinities for the long waves that roll along the edge. When the inner shallow reef area is calm, it has OK snorkeling, but there's always some current making it advisable only for advanced snorkelers.

When surf's up (especially in the summer), the water won't be very clear anyway, even if it's calmer near shore.

GETTING THERE   On Highway 50, between Waimea and Hanapepe (see map, page 171), you'll find the little town of Pākalā with beach along the south side of town. Public access is near the bridge. Park on either side of the road and take the un-marked path about 150 yards to the beach.

Lucy Wright Beach Park

Lucy Wright Beach Park isn't the best spot to snorkel due to the river run-off. While it provides good swimming in calm water, visibility tends to be very poor. The beach itself isn't the prettiest either, but it does have restrooms, showers and convenient parking.

GETTING THERE   Heading west on Highway 50, drive to the town of Waimea and cross the river. Here, head toward the beach to arrive at the park (see map, page 171). It's in front of the Russian fort.

manybar goatfish

West Area

The far western area of Kaua'i has a fifteen-mile long and broad sandy beach, but seldom offers safe snorkeling or swimming. The prevailing currents wrapping around Kaua'i come together offshore here to create some unusually strong and unpredictable currents.

Come for the beauty, the wide empty beaches and sand dunes, the warm dry weather and the view of Ni'ihau and Lehua islands at sunset. If you're getting way too much rain elsewhere on Kaua'i, you may find this corner of the island dry and appealing, but watch out for the hot sand.

The disadvantage is the time and effort it takes to get to the further locations (especially Polihale), as roads gradually get worse and sand increases. Those who drive out here consider that just part of the adventure, and a sure way to leave the crowds behind. Your rental car company will not be pleased if you get stuck out here on a sandy cane road.

You won't find accommodations, golf courses, or shopping in the west, just endless sand dunes all the way to the sharp cliffs of the Nā Pali Coast. A few tiny towns along Highway 50 do offer food and gas for the journey.

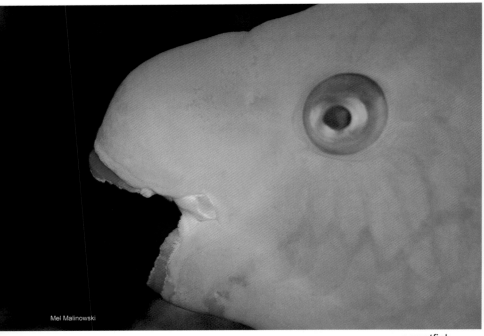

Mel Malinowski

parrotfish

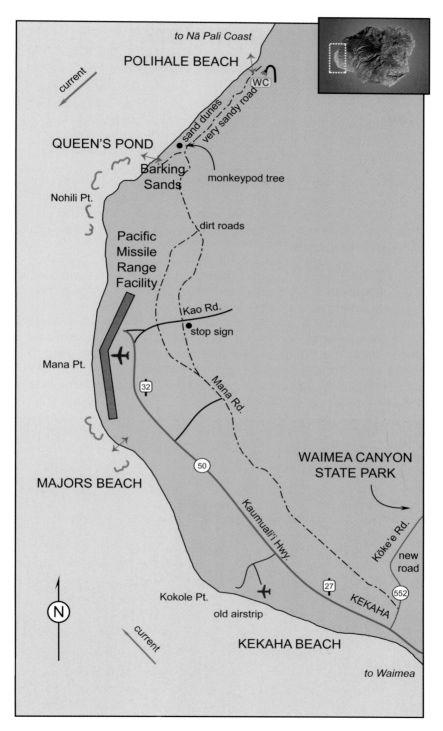

to Nā Pali Coast

POLIHALE BEACH

current

WC

sand dunes

very sandy road

QUEEN'S POND

Barking Sands

monkeypod tree

Nohili Pt.

dirt roads

Pacific Missile Range Facility

Kao Rd.

stop sign

Mana Pt.

32

Mana Rd.

WAIMEA CANYON STATE PARK

50

Kōke'e Rd.

MAJORS BEACH

Kaumuali'i Hwy.

new road

27

552

KEKAHA

N

current

Kokole Pt.

old airstrip

KEKAHA BEACH

to Waimea

179

Kekaha Beach Park

The beginning of a long stretch of sand that extends all the way to Polihale, this is a lovely beach, but it tends to have heavy surf. It's best to leave this one to the locals unless you get lucky and hit very calm conditions in the winter. It does have good snorkeling and swimming when unusually calm, but you'll need to pay close attention to currents and swells.

Facilities are located across the road from the center of the beach. You'll find a lifeguard station at the west end of the narrow park, with low sand dunes between the highway and the ocean. There is little or no shade along the beach, but it does have a good view of Niʻihau in the distance.

GETTING THERE   Along Highway 50 to the west of the town of Waimea, you'll find this long stretch of beach makai of the highway (on the ocean side)—see map, page 179. There's plenty of sand and facilities near the lifeguard station. The lifeguard looked rather lonely when we were last there, since the beach in front was utterly empty. Surfers will be well offshore when waves are good. If you're considering swimming or snorkeling here, stop by and check with the lifeguard about currents and swells. The current here usually sweeps west at a good clip.

Hawaiʻian day octopus

Barking Sands (Majors Beach)

Barking Sands refers to a great expanse of sand where the US tests some of its missiles. The Pacific Missile Range Facility has tightened its welcome of visitors due to security concerns. At the moment you need to apply for clearance and wait for a background check, so that rules this site out for tourists. Although the fifteen miles of sand are all part of Barking Sands, some people use the name to specifically refer to the Missile Facility area.

Typically, waves are kicking up making this a long dangerous beach complete with strong currents and undertow. One of the reasons this spot is so dangerous is that the open-ocean currents from the northeast divide to flow around Kaua'i, but come together again in the seas off Barking Sands to create some very rough and unpredictable conditions.

Barking Sands is a nice place to watch the sunset over Ni'ihau. The sand contains tiny holes that resonate when rubbed together. This works best when the sand is dry and is louder when a greater area is rubbed briskly. You'll definitely need shoes if you want to do this (or even traverse the sand) at midday because the sand here gets VERY hot. Some people have trouble getting the sand to bark, but at least it's fun to try.

You'll note that Kaua'i had an abundance of sand, particularly when compared to the other major Hawai'ian islands. What is doesn't have is the variety of sand colors: black, red, green, or even white. You'll find the more colorful sands mostly in the southern part of the Big Island, where more recent volcanic action supplies the materials. Kaua'i, being about five million years old, has well-mixed beaches of nearly identical caramel-colored sand.

GETTING THERE
Take Highway 50 west well past Waimea, then turn left at the entrance to the Pacific Missile Range Facility (see map, page 179). You will need prior clearance to get past the gate, so this only applies to residents with the proper permits in hand.

Queen's Pond

Not really worth a trip for snorkeling, Queen's Pond is a varying size area of shallow water just inland from the reef and breakers in the middle of a huge beach lined with sand dunes. This spot is hot, bare and beautiful in its own way, but has no facilities. The pond is sometimes too shallow to do anything except wade. It also requires a long hike over hot sand. By 9 a.m. it can be too hot to walk barefooted on the sand.

You may see 4WD vehicles down on the sand, but rental cars could easily get stuck and require an expensive tow. See our map for where to park and hike if you want to check out Queen's Pond.

While sand is shifting in the dunes, water is also rearranging with the seasons. Sand bars appear and disappear, while the bottom can drop off suddenly creating its own dangers. This can also affect the pond since it often gets hit by breakers.

GETTING THERE   As you head west on Highway 50 (see map, page 179), the highway eventually takes you to the Pacific Missile Range Facility. Near the entrance, jog to the right on Ka'o Road, then left, with signs marking the way on a dirt road to Polihale State Park. When this dirt road heads straight for the high dunes, you'll come to a huge monkeypod tree (3.3 miles from the end of the highway), where the road along the dunes splits in two directions. This is the only large tree in the area, so you aren't likely to miss it.

At the tree, go left for Queen's Pond and drive as far as seems prudent (only about .1 of a mile). Park along the road and walk over the sandiest stretch at the end. Follow any path up and over the tall dunes to your right for about 200 yards and you'll emerge on the vast sand beach.

Polihale State Park

This long stretch of sandy beach lined by hundred-foot tall sand dunes is located beyond the far western end of the highway. The park, at the edge of the Nā Pali Coast, is as far as you can go by car or even foot. It's hot here mid-days and afternoons, dry and rather stark. The park at the end of the dirt road does offer showers, restrooms, picnic tables, and even some shade. This is a good place to watch the sunset over Ni'ihau and Lehua Islands. When water is calm enough, snorkeling is OK at best, especially to the northwest beyond the end of the sand. Be cautious about conditions before going in.

This is one of the less hazardous stretches along the fifteen-mile long beach that wraps Kaua'i's western side. Be absolutely sure the current isn't too strong, however, before venturing out in the water here since there may not be anyone around to rescue you if you should get swept away. The current flows to your left rather than toward the Nā Pali Coast, which may be a plus. As always, don't go in the water without your fins, and don't snorkel alone!

Polihale State Park is about five miles beyond the end of the highway and the dirt road is quite slow, so allow extra time if you want to drive all this way. If you plan to stay till dark, make sure that you memorize the road carefully as you arrive, because a moonless night can make the dirt road hard to see and you won't want to be lost on any of the many side roads.

Come prepared for heat and sun. This is the hot, dry corner of Kaua'i at the end of fifteen miles of sand. Most of the natural water has long since been diverted for use in the sugar cane fields. Though sugar cane is gradually being replaced, water is unlikely to be returned. Bring plenty of your own.

If you're in Po'ipū during the summer, looking for a day's drive to the end of the road, you might want to consider Kē'ē Beach in the north instead. It's prettier and may not take any longer (depending on traffic). Besides, good snorkeling is more likely to be available at Kē'ē Beach in the summer. Winter, however, often brings large swells to the north making Polihale more appealing.

If you're looking for a place on Kaua'i to escape the rain, get warm (yes, Kaua'i can sometimes be cool in the winter), or escape the crowds, Polihale may be your best bet!

GETTING THERE

Follow Highway 50 west as far as it goes. When it reaches Ka'o Road at the Pacific Missile Range Facility (see map, page 179), it becomes dirt road, jogging right, then left at the light. Follow the signs to Polihale State Park as you continue for another five miles. When you come to the large monkeypod tree at the base of the dunes (about three miles from the highway), turn right and follow the dunes to Polihale, which is located at the very end of the road. Do watch the signs carefully because dirt cane roads lead off in several directions. These last few miles can be muddy after a heavy rain, so proceed with caution.

Nā Pali Coast Area

The spectacular Nā Pali Coast begins at Polihale on the west and continues to Kēʻē Beach at the end of the road in the northeast. The unbelievably near-vertical jagged cliffs of this coastline prevent roads of any sort. The only way to see this area up close without a helicopter is either by hiking the eleven-mile long difficult Kalalau Trail or arriving by water. Wonderful excursions are available, including comfortable catamarans, fast and bumpy Zodiac rafts, as well as kayaks when the water is calm enough. The larger catamarans traverse this area in all but the highest winter swells.

Only the smaller craft can land along the coast, because the reef is relatively shallow along the best beaches. Larger boats will be able to pass by for the gorgeous views of the saw-toothed peaks and tall waterfalls. When seas are somewhat calm, rafts and kayaks can enter the caves, duck under waterfalls, and land on the small, empty beaches, where Kauaʻi has two parks.

To see any of this coast by boat, you will need a guide of some sort since conditions can be treacherous at times. However, snorkeling can be surprisingly easy at the beaches protected by fringing reef.

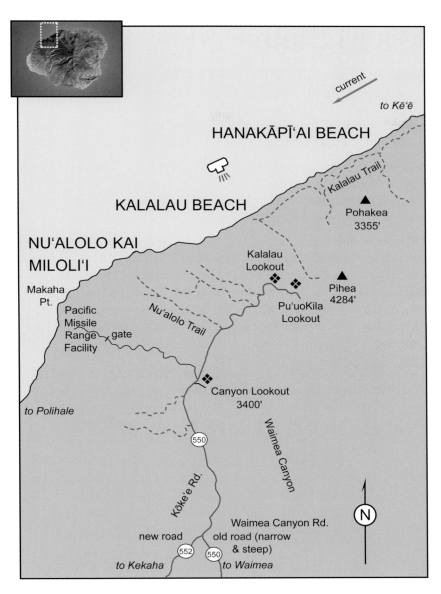

current

to Kē'ē

HANAKĀPĪ'AI BEACH

Kalalau Trail

▲ Pohakea
3355'

KALALAU BEACH

NU'ALOLO KAI
MILOLI'I

Kalalau
Lookout

▲ Pihea
4284'

Makaha
Pt.

Pu'uoKila
Lookout

Pacific
Missile
Range
Facility

Nu'alolo Trail

gate

Canyon Lookout
3400'

to Polihale

Waimea Canyon

(550)

Kōke'e Rd.

N

Waimea Canyon Rd.
new road   old road (narrow
(552) (550)   & steep)
to Kekaha   to Waimea

Potter's angelfish

185

Miloli'i State Park

Proceeding around the Nā Pali Coast for four miles from Polihale Park, we come to the first of several worthwhile snorkeling sites: Miloli'i State Park. The only access is by boat, unless you're a mountain climber and rappel down from the rugged peaks at about 5,000 foot altitude. That, however, is not permitted.

Miloli'i has a sandy beach and a fringing reef that extends about 250 feet seaward. It's a popular destination for excursions. Some provide snorkeling straight from their boat, while rafts and kayaks are small enough to drop you off on the shore.

Often calm due to the surrounding reef, Miloli'i offers fairly easy entry from the sand. The reef ranges from 2-15 feet under water, so you'll need very calm conditions to be comfortable. This makes for better snorkeling than swimming. It's a fun site to explore, if you stay well away from any big swells. Boats will drop you off here only if they have no doubts about safety. Currents are not a problem here on a calm day.

GETTING THERE   At the far southwest of the Nā Pali Coast, this beach is too isolated to access in any way but by boat.

Nu'alolo Kai State Park

Similar to Miloli'i and located to the northeast, this area offers better snorkeling than swimming and is one of the boat destinations. Nu'alolo Kai and Miloli'i both used to be fishing villages, and both contain interesting ruins. Although you can't see them from the beach, Nu'alolo Kai has terraced fields in the valley above.

The fringing reef at Nu'alolo Kai extends out about 500 feet and has a small boat channel in the center wide enough to accommodate kayaks or Zodiac rafts. The wide reef here offers some protection from waves most of the year, but that isn't enough in the heavy winter storms. When calm, the reef area is flat with little current. Winter brings a strong current out the channel. Entry from shore is easy if you don't mind pebbles and rocks.

When seas are very calm, this entire Nā Pali Coast offers superb kayaking. When a bit rougher, it offers quite a challenge. This whole coast provides some spectacular viewing either from a distance or

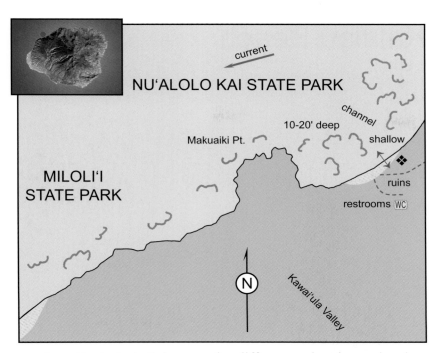

NU'ALOLO KAI STATE PARK

current

channel

10-20' deep

Makuaiki Pt.

shallow

ruins

restrooms WC

MILOLI'I
STATE PARK

N

Kawai'ula Valley

up close. Try to do both because the cliffs, caves, beaches and rocky cliffs can best be seen and explored up close, while the lush valleys, saw-toothed mountain ranges, and high waterfalls can best be viewed from a bit further out to sea or by helicopter.

These Nā Pali beaches, lovely as they may be, attract insects and mice, who thrive by eating what tourists leave behind. When winter swells arrive, snorkeling isn't the best because towering waves often crash against these cliffs.

However, as a setting for a calm snorkel in good weather, what could be better? Even if you don't see too much underwater, you can glance up at the dramatic green mountains in the background. A thoroughly enjoyable way to spend the day! Amenities include restrooms set back from the rocky beach, a couple of covered picnic tables and a short hike to the ruins and heiau. Take care to avoid stepping in the smelly jackfruit that fall onto the trail and quickly rot (picturesquely, of course).

GETTING THERE

Nu'alolo Kai State Park is best accessed by boat due to the surrounding steep cliffs, although it is possible to hike down on the Nu'alolo Trail from Kōke'e Road. Experts only. Not a realistic option for most tourists.

Kalalau Beach

This incredibly lovely beach at the foot of the steep Kalalau Valley is located at the end of the Kalalau Trail, about eleven miles along the coast from the start at Kē'ē Beach. Camping is allowed here on the beach near the dunes, but with permits only and there's a long waiting list for these. A ranger does indeed enforce the rules, especially if you're down on the beach in plain sight. They may confiscate your gear!

While it can sometimes be calm and safe, the surf is often very rough on the western side of Kaua'i. When breakers hit the beach, they are accompanied by plenty of undertow as well as currents that can and do sweep people away. The rip current is most often found in the center of the beach. There is no protecting reef at this beach.

Other than the eleven-mile difficult hike (where you need to either bring drinking water or treat it), access is only possible by boat. Kayakers sometimes come ashore here when weather permits, but it isn't a snorkeling destination for the excursions.

GETTING THERE   Kalalau Beach is an oasis located at the end of the spectacular Kalalau Trail after a difficult eleven-mile hike from Kē'ē Beach in northern Kaua'i (see map, page 151). This is not a hike for day-trippers.

You can camp with permit only, but these fill a year or more ahead. You'll need to bring or treat any fresh water along the coast. Permits are strictly enforced by a reputedly ever-present ranger.

Hanakāpī'ai Beach

For those who don't want to hike eleven challenging miles to Kalalau Beach, Hanakāpī'ai Beach is only two miles from the start of Kalalau Trail at Kē'ē Beach and takes about one and a half hours each way.

This is a steep, and usually slippery, two miles, so most people arrive at the beach ready to hop in the water. Think again and check out the waves, then opt to splash around in the shallow water protected by a sand bar. Hikers with any energy left can take another tough two-mile hike up to the waterfall.

More folks have drowned at this beach than any other in Kaua'i because it lacks a protecting reef and nearly always has a rip current. Tourists (usually over-confident young men) get in trouble here frequently. Once you have been pulled out away from shore, it can be difficult or impossible to return and there's no handy phone for calling the coast guard, or anyone around to help you.

Needless to say, we don't recommend snorkeling here. We do recommend the dramatic and downright breathtaking trail up and down the edge of the Nā Pali Coast, but try to hike when it hasn't been raining too heavily. Slippery mud does nothing to ease the hike. As you wind up and down the dramatic coast, take time to enjoy the uniquely beautiful view.

GETTING THERE   If you want a taste of the dramatic and gorgeous Kalalau Trail, Hanakāpī'ai Beach is just two miles from Kē'ē Beach in northwestern Kaua'i (see map, page 45). This is a rugged, but spectacular trail to a lovely beach, where you definitely should not swim or snorkel due to the danger of waves and currents. Excursions often follow the Nā Pali Coast to show you the view, but are unlikely to stop here because there are plenty of safer spots along the Nā Pali Coast.

Ni'ihau and Lehua

Holoholo Charters

Three quarters of a mile from the northern coast of Ni'ihau Island, you'll find some superb snorkeling at Lehua Island. For those who have been to Molokini (near Maui), Lehua is a similar, bare crescent-shaped rim of a volcanic island, composed of tuff, which is pressed volcanic ash. The best snorkeling is usually on the back at the southwestern corner making the snorkeling quite different from the inside of Molokini. And no crowds at all!

Lehua Island is accessible by boat only and offers some of the clearest water in Hawai'i—a must-see destination for dedicated snorkelers. The back of the island is protected from big northern swells and is close enough to Ni'ihau to gain protection from southern swell. The exact site must be chosen by the captain, but you're likely to find a spot that offers a shallow reef with steep drop-off into the big blue sea.

To give you a brief example of what awaits at Lehua, in one day we saw large schools of pyramid, milletseed, and pennant butterflyfish,

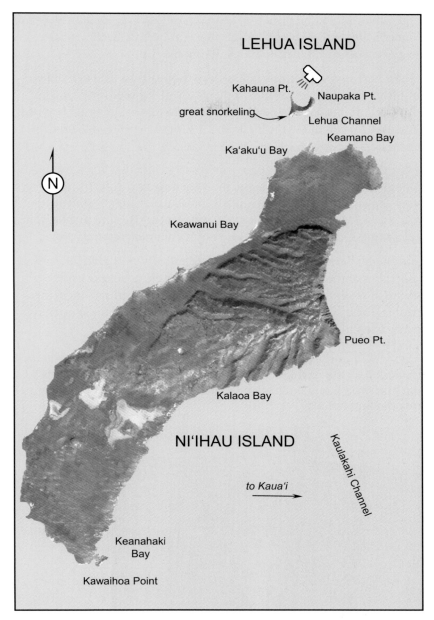

LEHUA ISLAND

Kahauna Pt.

Naupaka Pt.

great snorkeling

Lehua Channel

Keamano Bay

Ka'aku'u Bay

Keawanui Bay

N

Pueo Pt.

Kalaoa Bay

NI'IHAU ISLAND

Kaulakahi Channel

to Kaua'i

Keanahaki Bay

Kawaihoa Point

all sorts of other butterflyfish including raccoon, fourspot, longnose and the saddleback. Wrasses and tangs were abundant and we spotted bandit angelfish, seldom seen while snorkeling elsewhere in Hawai'i. During one trip, we snorkeled with manta rays, a very curious monk seal, and a five foot Galapagos shark. Dolphins cavorted nearby,

191

and brown-footed boobies flew overhead. If lucky, you may also see humpback whales (December through April only), turtles, and/or huge schools of spinner dolphins during the trip.

Water here is crystal clear with a steep drop-off, so the deep blues of the open ocean set off the bright colors of the reef fish. The reef itself is still in excellent condition. Granted this is a long trip by boat, especially when the sea is high, and it's more expensive than most excursions (see page 194).

Even though we didn't go on a particularly calm day, it's a trip we would have happily taken again the very next day. A fast, smooth, very seaworthy boat is preferable because the channel between Kaua'i and Ni'ihau is about twenty miles wide. Be sure to take your seasickness remedy if needed (see our recommendation on page 21).

Although all beaches in Hawai'i are technically available for public use, the island of Ni'ihau has managed to prevent access while trying to retain the traditional isolation for its Hawai'ian-speaking people. Dive boats go to many sites near the island, but do not have permission to go on land.

GETTING THERE   While access to Ni'ihau itself is forbidden, boats can lie offshore and snorkel. This is a twenty-mile trip from Port Allen, but it's a beautiful twenty miles and we highly recommend the trip.

a snorkeling site at Lehua Island

spotted pufferfish

193

EXCURSIONS

HOLOHOLO CHARTERS

One of Kaua'i's premier excursions, Holoholo is extremely popular for good reason. For a rare chance to snorkel in a pristine environment, try their trip to Lehua Island off the north coast of Ni'ihau. You'll have to be in Port Allen at 6 a.m. to sign in and join your fellow sleepy passengers, but a full continental breakfast with cinnamon rolls and fruit will be waiting on board the catamaran.

The boat heads west and north following Kaua'i's coast past Barking Sands and Polihale. At that point you'll begin the dramatic Nā Pali Coast portion of the trip. We saw tall waterfalls, lush deep valleys, the fabled saw-toothed ridges, and stopped to spend some time watching a large pod of spinner dolphins (at least two hundred). They swam near the boat, slapped their fins and a few treated us to a display of spinning jumps.

If the time of year is right, there's a chance of seeing whales and manta rays on the trip. Holoholo even stopped to see a whale shark a couple of weeks before our trip. Now that one was a thrill for the crew and some lucky passengers!

Then, it was onward to Lehua Island, a small bare crescent-shaped crater within a mile of Ni'ihau Island. Water here is crystal-clear, the snorkeling site well-protected, and both coral and fish are abundant For those who have been to Molokini, off Maui, Lehua is a similar volcanic crater, but the calm snorkeling here is on the back, where the steep drop-off is quite dramatic.

Holoholo provides all snorkeling equipment and various type of floats including "noodles" for novice snorkelers. The area we tried had a flat shallow reef near shore with a steep drop-off (30-70 feet) where fish congregated in the nutrient-rich waters. At the edge we could watch lovely colorful reef fish with the deepest indigo water in the background while pelagic fish passed by outside the reef.

While we could've stayed in the water all day, it was eventually time to board for lunch of make-your-own deli sandwiches, salads, fruit and a variety of drinks (including beer, now that the snorkeling time was finished).

Along the back of Lehua, we proceeded to Keyhole Rock (a popular photo op), had a good view of Niʻihau from the boat, then back across the channel—ending the trip with always-available drinks and lots of chocolate chip macadamia nut cookies.

This is open ocean between the islands, so do take your seasickness remedy if needed. See our recommendation on page 21 because you don't want a silly thing like seasickness to spoil this magical day.

We were surprised to learn that Holoholo doesn't have to cancel often. South swells had been somewhat high before we went, but the trip was quite smooth in this fast and comfortable catamaran. When out in the open channel, do take their words of caution and make use of the many guard-rails to hold on at all times you're not in a seat.

Holoholo Charters   800-848-6130

www.holoholocharters.com   808-335-0815

KAUAʻI SEA TOURS

Kauaʻi Sea Tours offers several options for excursions along the Nā Pali Coast. We tried both the zodiac-type raft with eight passengers and Lucky Lady, a catamaran holding about fifty people.

Take the raft for maximum adventure. It's guaranteed to be bumpy, wet, thrilling, with full exposure to the sun. They don't take anyone who is pregnant or has serious back or neck trouble—for obvious reasons. If you want an easy trip, choose the bigger boat, but for a ton of fun, nothing beats the raft if you're rough and tough enough.

The rafting trip begins with coffee and sweet rolls in the office. Don't forget to use the restroom, as it is several hours before any stop. There are no restrooms on board, so you need to ask for a stop and hop in the water to relieve yourself. We set out from Port Allen with stops along the way to see dolphins and turtles. At the start of the Nā Pali Coast we zipped from valley to cave to cliff. At times the raft entered smallish caves, drove under a waterfall, and explored many of the nooks and crannies along this gorgeous coastline.

One of more interesting stops was in a cave where the entire top opened up to the sky. The cliffs along the side of the cave were about sixty feet straight up. While the rafts can explore this coastline most of the year, they can only enter the caves when north swells aren't too high, and are less likely to encounter such good conditions during winter storms.

The narration was fascinating, though a little hard to hear when the raft was on the move—especially from the back of the raft. Eventually we returned to Nu'alolo Kai Beach. The raft edged right in close to shore, where we enjoyed the picnic lunches at the tables set in a covered shelter. Quite a picturesque picnicing spot! Snorkeling was in a calm area right in front with relatively easy entry from the shore. The reef here is five to fifteen feet deep with plenty of space to wander. This isn't a spectacular site with big numbers of fish, but we had excellent views of some very colorful ones. If you look very close, you might also see octopuses here.

For a more sedate trip, try the Lucky Lady, a comfortable boat with a nice set-up for snorkelers to enter the water. They too provide all equipment as well as breakfast and lunch onboard. They slice through the swells in the channel, but still provided enough bounce

Dive Boats

PADI and NAUI attempt to regulate the diving industry with strict rules, since there are serious risks involved. No one is allowed to dive without certification (a C Card). Anyone who wants to dive without proper training is certainly a fool, and the shops who will take such rash people out are equally foolish.

We have seen excursions all over the world offering to take people down without proof of certification. This is not the mark of the highest level of safety consciousness. Keep in mind that other advice and services from such operators may be similarly casual. Always take extra care with any rental equipment.

When their business is slow, some take divers (or snorkelers) to sites they can't handle. On the better snorkeling excursions, they keep a close eye on all their charges, so it's like having a lifeguard along.

Tagging along with a dive boat, you may find yourself on the surface as a snorkeler in much rougher conditions than the divers sixty feet beneath you. You'll need to rely on a buddy since the crew is usually more focused on the divers. It's a good idea to ask in advance whether good snorkeling is possible at the particular dive site they are planning for that day.

in the front of the boat, where they allowed some brave passengers to sit on the "trampoline" and get a wild ride on their way back to port, getting drenched by waves now and then—to the great amusement of the whole group.

For snorkeling, the Lucky Lady took us to Miloli'i along the cliffs of the Nā Pali Coast. If you are an experienced snorkeler and have a chance, sign up to go one cove further on their raft (which makes a rendezvous here with Lucky Lady) because the snorkeling is a bit better at Nu'alolo Kai Beach. That's also an interesting way to have a comfortable ride up, and a touch of rafting adventure, too.

Beginners will probably want to stay with the Lucky Lady. The staff is alert to provide whatever it takes to make you comfortable in the water and out. For first-time snorkelers, you won't find a boat with a better arrangement for entry and exit.

Depending on the season, Sea Tours offers 4, 5, or 6 hour snorkeling trips as well as sunset excursions and whale watching.

Kaua'i Sea Tours   800-733-7997
www.kauaiseatours.com   808-335-5309

SEA FUN KAUA'I

While this company offers a variety of trips around Kaua'i, we've sampled just their snorkeling trip. This half-day shore-based trip will vary the location depending on current ocean conditions. They pick you at most hotels, and provide all gear, snacks and lunch.

Each tour is led by an expert with knowledge of the area to be snorkeled. They welcome non-swimmers and have plenty of aids such as float boards if needed. The whole group snorkels together with more advanced snorkelers allowed to explore nearby. Our snorkel van headed to Tunnels on a fairly calm day, spending a full two hours in the water as the group slowly drifted along the reef. After our snorkel, the van met us at the edge of the sand and gave us all a ride down to Hā'ena State Park for showers and lunch.

This is a good way for beginners (especially children) to learn to snorkel and head out to deeper water with supervision. The leader of our group was extremely patient and made sure that everyone was comfortable. Worth checking out, especially if being in a group makes you more comfortable in the water.

Sea Fun Kaua'i   808-245-6400

Marine Life

The coral reef supports tremendous diversity in a small space. On a healthy reef, you've never seen everything, because of the boggling variety of species, as well as changes from day to day and changes from day to night. The reef functions much like the oasis in the desert providing food (more abundant than the open ocean) and shelter from predators. Only the wild rain forests can compare with the reef in complexity.

In Hawai'i the reef coral itself is less spectacular than in warmer waters of the world. This is counterbalanced by the colorful and abundant fish, which provide quite a show.

There are excellent color fish identification cards available in bookstores and dive shops. We particularly like the ones published by Natural World Press. There are also many good marine life books that give far more detailed descriptions of each creature than we attempt in these brief notes.

Hawai'ian day octopus

Hawai'ian night octopus

OCTOPUS

Some varieties of octopuses hide during the day while others hunt by day. They eat shrimp, fish, crabs, and mollusks—you should eat so well! Octopuses have strong "beaks" and can bite humans, so it's safer to not handle them.

Being mollusks without shells, they must rely on speed, cunning and camouflage to escape danger. Octopuses are capable of imitating a flashing sign, or changing their color and texture to match their surroundings in an instant. This makes them very hard to spot, even when they're hiding in plain sight—usually on the bottom or on rocks. They also squirt ink to confuse predators. They only live about two years.

Just because you haven't seen one does not mean they aren't there. Go slow and watch carefully for a rock or coral that moves. It may take you some time to find one (weeks? months?) but when you do, it is a real thrill.

SHRIMP

In all kinds, colors, and sizes, they like to hide in rocks and coral—often living symbiotically with the coral. They are difficult to spot during the daytime, but at night you will notice lots of tiny pairs of eyes reflected in the flashlight beam. Most are fairly small and well-disguised.

banded coral shrimp

Some examples include: the harlequin shrimp (brightly colored) that eat sea stars, the banded coral shrimp (found all over the world), and numerous tiny shrimp that you won't see without magnification.

SEA URCHINS

Concealed tube feet allow urchins to move around in their hunt for algae. The collector urchin has pebbles and bits of coral attached for camouflage. These urchins are quite common in Hawai'i, and have no hazardous spines.

Beware of purple-black urchins with long spines. These are common in shallow water at certain beaches. It's not the long spines that get you, it's the razor-sharp ones hidden beneath. The bright red pencil sea urchin is common and easy to spot. Although large, its spines aren't nearly sharp enough to be a problem for people. The spines can actually be used for chalk.

banded sea urchin

SEA STARS

brittle star

Abundant, but not seen much by snorkelers. The crown of thorns sea star, which can be such a devastator of coral reefs, is found in Hawai'i, but not in large numbers like the South Pacific. Sea stars firmly grasp their prey with strong suction cups, and then eat at their leisure.

RAYS

manta ray

Manta rays (large plankton-eaters) use two flaps to guide plankton into their huge efficient mouths. Mantas often grow to be two meters from wing-tip to wing-tip, and can weigh 300 pounds. They can't sting, but are large enough to bump hard.

Mantas feed at night by doing forward rolls in the water with mouths wide open. Lights will attract plankton which appeal to the manta rays. Dive boats can easily attract manta rays with their bright lights making the night trips very exciting.

Another beautiful ray, the spotted eagle ray, can sometimes be seen cruising the bottom for food and can grow to be seven feet across. They have a dark back with lots of small white dots and an extremely

spotted eagle ray

long tail. Their fins function more like wings to enable them to seem to "fly" along rather than swimming.

Common sting rays prefer the sandy bottom and usually stay in calm, shallow, warmer water.

EELS

Many types of moray eels abound among the reefs of Kaua'i. They can easily grow up to two meters long. While you may not see any on a given day, you can be sure they are all around the reef hiding in crevices.

whitemouth moray eel

Varieties of moray found in Hawai'i include undulated, whitemouth, snowflake, zebra (black and white stripes), wavy-lined, mottled, and dragon moray (often reddish-brown with distinct white spots of differing sizes).

Morays prefer to hide in holes during the day. If out cruising, they often find a nearby hole when spotting a snorkeler. When they stick out their heads and breathe, their teeth are most impressive.

undulated moray eel

Eels generally have no interest in eating snorkelers, other than very pushy and annoying ones, while they are quite able to swallow a fairly large fish. Please avoid putting your hands into reef crevices, since this is a great way to spend the afternoon getting stitches.

TRUMPETFISH

These long, skinny fish can change color, often bright yellow, light green with shaded bars, or light blue—and will change color in front of your eyes. They sometimes hang upright to blend with their

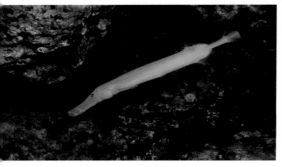

environment, lying in wait to suck in their prey. They also shadow other fish and change their color to sneak up on prey—even at a cleaning station.

trumpetfish

They do eat throughout the day, which is unusual for fish-eaters, who usually eat at dawn or dusk. Trumpetfish are quite

common in Kaua'i and often seen hanging out alone. Some grow to more than one meter long, although you will usually see only the smaller ones.

Cornetfish are similar to trumpetfish in shape and size, but have a distinctive thin filament extending from the center of the tail. Sometimes small cornetfish can be seen in big groups. Adults can be larger than trumpetfish and can also change color.

cornetfish

NEEDLEFISH

These pointed, common silvery-blue fish like swimming very near the surface, usually in schools—occasionally leaping from the water. All types of needlefish are long and skinny as their name implies, and grow to as much as one to two feet long. Color and markings vary, but the long narrow shape is distinctive and hard to mistake. They're usually bluish on top, and translucent below for camouflage.

BUTTERFLYFISH

Butterflyfish are beautiful, colorful, abundant and varied in Hawai'i. They have incredible coloration, typically bright yellow, white, orange, black, and sometimes a little blue or red. They hang out near coral, eating algae, sponges, tube worms and very small coral polyps.

ornate butterflyfish

No one really understands the purpose of their beautiful colors, but many have speculated. Perhaps they serve territorial or mating needs.

threadfin butterflyfish

Juveniles are often distinctly different in coloring. Bizarre patterns may confuse predators — especially since they can pivot fast. Bars may help some hide, while stripes are seen more in faster fish. Black lines across the eyes and spots near the tail may also confuse predators.

multiband butterflyfish

Butterflyfish are often seen in pairs remaining together for up to three years. They're all delightful to watch. Hovering and turning are more important to them than speed since they stay near shelter of the reef and catch a quick meal — like a tube worm.

longnose butterflyfish

203

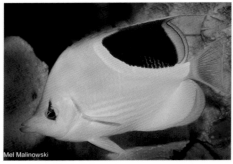
saddleback butterflyfish

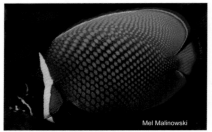
reticulated butterflyfish

fourspot butterflyfish

teardrop butterflyfish

The ones you are most likely to see while snorkeling in Hawai'i include: raccoon (reminding you of the face of the animal), ornate (with bright orange lines making it easy to spot), threadfin (with diagonal lines), saddleback (fairly rare), lemon (very tiny), bluestripe (a beautiful one found only in Hawai'i), fourspot, milletseed, teardrop, and forceps (also called longnose).

The lined butterflyfish is the largest variety found in Hawai'i. The reticulated, often found in the surge zone, are not common, but are particularly beautiful. The smaller ovals (found in pairs scattered around on most reefs) seem to glow from within, especially on a sunny day.

Many butterflyfish have black spots across the eyes and near the tail—perhaps to confuse a predator about which way they're headed. Watch and they may confuse you too.

Most butterflyfish are common near the reef and pay little attention to snorkelers so they're fun to watch and often easy to identify with their distinctive markings.

PARROTFISH

Among the most dramatically colored fish on the reef, male parrotfish are blue, green, turquoise, yellow, lavender, and/or orange with endless variations of these colors. Females tend to be a more drab reddish brown. No two are alike. Parrotfish are very beautiful, with artistic, abstract markings.

female parrotfish

These fish change colors at different times in their lives and can also change sex as needed. They can be quite large (up to one meter).

male parrotfish

Patient grazers, they spend countless hours scraping algae from dead coral with their large, beak-like teeth, and create tons of white sand in the process. Most prefer to zoom away from snorkelers, but you'll see them passing gracefully by and will hear them crunching away at the coral. Unfortunately they are heavily fished and less numerous lately.

Picasso (lagoon) triggerfish

TRIGGERFISH

Fond of sea urchins as a main course, triggerfish graze during the day on algae, worms and other small items.

Varieties include the Picasso (wildly colorful—quite rare at many sites, but worth watching for), reef (the Hawai'ian state fish), pinktail (easy to identify with its black body, white fins and pink tail), black (common, distinctive white lines between body and fins). The checkerboard triggerfish has a pink tail, yellow-edged fins, and blue stripes on its face. Triggerfish are beautiful and fascinating to watch.

lei triggerfish

205

pinktail triggerfish

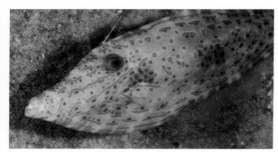
scrawled filefish

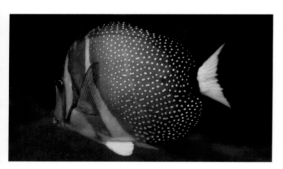
spotted surgeonfish

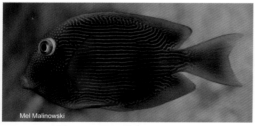
goldrim surgeonfish

FILEFISH

The scrawled filefish has blue scribbles and brown dots over its olive green body. Quite large, up to one meter, often in pairs, but seen occasionally in groups.

A filefish will often turn its body flat to your view, and raise its top spine in order to impress you. This lets you have a great close-up view — and a perfect photo opportunity.

SURGEONFISH

Razor-sharp fin-like spines on each side of the tail are the hallmark of this fish, quite common in Hawai'i. These spines provide excellent defense, but aren't needed to fend off tourists since surgeonfish can easily swim away.

Varieties includes the orangeband surgeonfish (with distinctive long, bright orange marks on the side), as well as the Achilles tang (also called naso tang), which has bright orange spots surrounding the spines near the orange tail. The common yellow tang is completely yellow and smaller. The sailfin tang has dramatic vertical markings. It's less common, but easy to identify.

WRASSES

Wrasses are amazingly bright and multicolored fish. Hawai'ian cleaner wrasses set themselves up for business and operate cleaning stations, where they clean much larger fish without having to worry about becoming dinner. They eat parasites, and provide an improbable reef service in the process. Perhaps their bright colors serve as neon signs to advertise their services. Hang out near their cleaning stations for excellent fish viewing. In Hawai'i, the tiny cleaner wrasse (about two inches) is neon yellow, purple-blue and black.

Other wrasses are larger including the dazzling yellowtail (up to 15 inches), which is covered with glowing blue spots, many stripes, and a bright yellow tail. The juvenile yellowtail is bright orange with a few big white spots, looking completely different from the adult.

Another large wrasse, the saddleback, is endemic to Hawai'i. It is bright blue, with green, orange and white markings. Wrasses are closely related to parrotfish, but usually smaller.

eyestripe surgeonfish

yellowtail coris

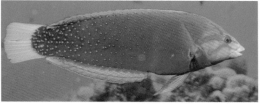
saddle wrasse

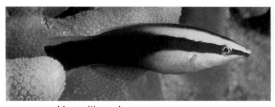
Hawai'ian cleaner wrasse

male bird wrasse

SCORPIONFISH

Hawai'ian turkeyfish

Mel Malinowski

The Hawai'ian turkeyfish is very colorful example, with feather-like multicolored spines. Beware of their poisonous spines, though! Don't even think about touching a scorpionfish, and try to avoid accidentally stepping on one.

This varied group of exotic fish includes the bright red Hawai'ian turkeyfish, sometimes called a lionfish.

Other scorpionfish are so well-camouflaged that they are hard to see. They just lurk on the bottom blending in well with the sand and coral. If you see one, count yourself lucky, but don't step on it!

PUFFERFISH

male spotted toby

Pufferfish (and the related trunkfish) swim slowly due to their boxy shape, so need more protection. Puffers can blow up like prickly balloons when threatened.

Two kinds are common in sheltered areas: porcupine (displaying spines when inflated), and spotted trunkfish, boxfish and tobies (often brown or black with lots of white dots). Most tend to prefer to escape under the coral, although some seem unafraid of snorkelers and even curious. You may spot a big porcupine face peering out from under coral (giving the appearance of a much larger fish such as a shark).

The small spotted toby is common over the reef. The female is brown

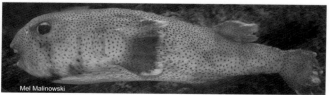

Mel Malinowski

with white spots and the male is a beautiful dark blue with orange spots.

porcupinefish

SHARKS

Although sharks have quite a reputation for teeth rather than brains, they are unquestionably survivors, having been around for about 300 million years.

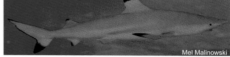

This is an extremely successful species with keen hearing, smell, sight and ability to detect electrical signals through the

blacktip reefshark

water. They swim with a side-to-side motion, which does not make them speedy by ocean standards.

When snorkeling you are unlikely to spot any shark except the whitetip or blacktip hanging around shallow water. Plenty of larger species pass by Hawai'i, but tend to prefer the deeper waters further out in the channels.

DOLPHINS

Spinner dolphins are frequently seen in large schools (at least 200). They swim as small family groups within these schools, and often swim fast, leaping out of the water to spin in the air. They tend to hang out in certain locations, so you can search for them if you like.

spinner dolphins

Spinners are a bit sleeker than other dolphins and arrive at large bays to rest during the day. Dolphins sleep on one side at a time, so they can swim while resting.

Bottlenose dolphins often approach fast-moving boats, and it is a great thrill to watch them race along just in front of the bow of your boat, jumping in and out of the water with grace and easy speed.

Beaked and spotted dolphins are also commonly seen in the waters off Hawai'i.

bottlenose dolphins

SEA TURTLES

Green sea turtles (the most common in Hawai'i) are becoming more plentiful lately and seem to be less concerned about snorkelers.

Sea turtles are often seen in pairs. Larger specimens (often seen at The Cliffs or Hō'ai Bay) can be up to 100 years old, and tend to be docile and unafraid. You'll often see them resting on the bottom in about ten to twenty feet of water during the day. They sometimes let you swim as close as you like, but it's best not to hover over them because they do need to come up for air. Just before dusk, they often hunt for algae along the lava coastline and don't seem to mind being

tumbled against the sharp rocky shore.

Do not disturb these graceful creatures, so they can remain unafraid to swim among snorkelers. In Hawai'i it is against the law to touch or harass sea turtles. Enjoy, but don't crowd them.

WHALES

Humpback whales migrate here to breed in winter, around early December through April. Humpbacks come quite close to the coast, where you can watch whole families. They are so large that you can often easily see them spouting and breaching. Their great size never fails to impress, as does their fluid, seemingly effortless graceful movement in the water. Many excursions offer whale-watching trips during the winter season.

humpback whale

211

Weather

All islands have a windward side, which is wetter, and a leeward side which is drier. In Hawai'i, the northeast is windward and hence wet, and the southwest is leeward, or kona, and hence drier and sunnier. Waves from afar tend to arrive from the north in winter and from the south in summer, although this pattern changes often.

Hawai'i gets most of its rain in the winter. The most severe storms (called kona), however, come from the south and can even bring hurricanes in the summer. Temperatures tend to be very mild year-round, yet there is variety around Kaua'i on any day of the year. There are days when you could tan in Po'ipū in the morning, drive up to cool Kōke'e Park later, while rain continues in Hanalei. Summer temperatures are five to eight degrees F warmer than winter.

Evaporating moisture from the ocean forms clouds. As the clouds rise over the mountains, they cool, and the condensing moisture becomes rain. Mount Wai'ale'ale receives 500 inches of rain a year, while Po'ipū only gets about 20 inches.

Having lost most of their moisture in passing over the mountains, the clouds have little left for the leeward side — so it is in the rain shadow of the mountains. The leeward weather is therefore often sunny. Waikīkī, Po'ipū, Kā'anapali, and Kona are all in rain shadows. On Kaua'i, if you get stuck with heavy rains in Hanalei, just head for Po'ipū to find the sun.

Changeable is the word for Kaua'i's weather — not just between areas, but also rapidly changeable in any given place. The trade winds blow about 90% of the time in the summer and about 50% in the winter. They tend to be stronger in the afternoon and are stronger on Kaua'i than the other Hawai'ian islands.

The windward or northeastern coasts have much more rain, wind and waves — something important to remember when snorkeling.

Seasonal Changes

Kaua'i has much milder weather than the continental United States, yet it is has seasons you might call winter, spring and summer. At 20°N Latitude, there are nearly 2 1/2 hours more sun in midsummer than in midwinter, which is 21% more. But the moderating effect of the ocean keeps temperature swings quite moderate.

Winter is the cooler, wetter season. Cooler is a relative term, as the average high temperature in winter falls to a brisk 80° F, as opposed to a summer average high of 88° F. Water temperature in winter falls to around 72° F, and at times, wind, rain and cooler air temperatures can temper your desire to splash around in the water. Winter usually begins in mid-November, with the start of winter storms from the north-northwest. This is the start of the large wave season on the north coast. Winter tails off in mid-March.

Spring really is just the transition from winter to summer, and is marked by the end of winter storms in mid-March. Hours of sunshine go up, especially on the west, leeward side of the island. This can be a very pleasant time of year. Spring transitions into summer in May.

Summer begins in May, as the weather warms, and the rains slacken. Trade winds temper the heat and humidity almost all the time. This is prime sunning and play time. An occasional tropical storm or hurricane can come through, and swells can roll in from the south. The heat softens in October as summer draws to an end.

Month by Month

JANUARY   This month offers an opportunity for the wettest weather all year. It's also one of the coolest. Large surf can often pound the north and west exposed beaches of Kaua'i.

FEBRUARY   Just as cool, the surf continues to hit the north and west exposed beaches, although storms are a bit less frequent than January.

MARCH   The weather starts to improve with fewer storms, especially in the west.

APRIL   Spring arrives early, so warm weather begins during this month. Expect a few late swells.

MAY   Summer is already arriving—especially in the south and west. This tends to be a trouble-free month.

JUNE   This offers very warm and dry weather with plenty of sun. Fortunately the winds blow nearly every day.

JULY   Much the same as June, except that storms in the South Pacific begin at this time. They hit beaches exposed to the south.

AUGUST	Another warm month, occasional big waves can hit the southern exposed beaches.
SEPTEMBER	This last month of summer can sometimes be the hottest and most humid. Hurricanes can strike Kaua'i, and are most common this month. Most will miss the islands, but bring muggy weather. 'Iniki, however, brought widespread damage to Kaua'i.
OCTOBER	Milder weather begins this month with the start of storms arriving from the north.
NOVEMBER	Sometimes the first real winter storms arrive and they can be somewhat cool.
DECEMBER	This is winter with frequent storms and wind bringing big waves to the exposed northern and western beaches. However, even this month can be clear and warm between storms.

Coolest month:	February
Hottest month:	September
Rainiest month:	January
Driest month:	June
Coolest water:	December-April
Warmest water:	August-September

Tide

Tides are very slight in Kaua'i, with the average difference between high and low only two to three feet max. It's a good idea to know which way the tide is going because tidal flow does affect the currents. If the tide is going out, you might want to avoid snorkeling in places where water is already shallow or currents tend to sweep out of a bay, often the center, or a gap in the reef (see Understanding waves, page 27). Tides matter more in Kaua'i than the other islands.

Water Temperature

On the surface, the water in Kaua'i gets as low as 72° F (22° C) in March to as high as 80° F (27° C) in September. Sheltered bays can be a bit warmer, while deeper or rough water can be surprisingly cool. Kaua'i, being furthest north of the main islands, is typically a little cooler than the other main islands. If you happen to be slender, no longer young, or from a moderate climate, this can seem cooler than you might like—especially if you like to snorkel for hours.

Hurricane

Summer is possible hurricane season, but it is also the time when weather is typically excellent. While the storms don't last long, they can be terribly destructive. Hurricanes can bring amazingly heavy rain and winds to the islands. Any could receive a direct hit, which happened when Hurricanes 'Iwa (1982) and later much stronger 'Iniki (see page 87) clobbered Kaua'i. Very few hurricanes ever actually hit Hawai'i, fortunately.

Tsunami

Huge waves can be triggered by earthquakes either in the islands or far across the Pacific. Though quite rare, separated by decades usually, they've hit Hawai'i a number of times, more often from the north. Depending on the exact direction, they can directly hit a valley and really wipe it out and rinse it clean. It is better to not be there when this happens. Groups of tsunami waves are often spaced as far as fifteen to twenty minutes apart, and often catch unsuspecting folks who go down to the beach too soon.

There's likely to be plenty of warning due to ever-vigilant earthquake monitoring equipment, elaborate modeling systems, and large numbers of beach-side tsunami warning sirens. Still, authorities prefer to warn of every possible tsunami just to be safe. It doesn't pay to ignore warnings just because the sea appears calm. If a major earthquake strikes while you're visiting, it's a good idea to head rapidly for high ground. Leave bays or valleys which can act to funnel the effects of a large wave.

Due the superior forecasting and warning systems now in place, Hawai'i is unlikely to ever experience the unforewarned destruction of the great Indonesian tsunami of December 26, 2004. To help insure that this is so, if you hear a loud warning siren, and don't have very good reason to know it is just a test, play it safe and leave the beach immediately for high ground.

Language

English is now the official language of the islands of Hawai'i (except for the island of Ni'ihau.) However, most place names and lots of slang are Hawai'ian, so it's helpful to at least be able to pronounce enough to be understood. It's a very straight-forward phonetic language: each letter is usually pronounced just one way. The long place names aren't nearly so daunting when you have learned the system.

All syllables end with a vowel. When the missionaries attempted to write this oral language, they used only seven consonants (h,k,l,m,n,p,w). However, there is actually an eighth consonant in spoken Hawai'ian, the glottal stop (called an 'okina)—marked by the '. This is not the same as an apostrophe: '.When you say 'Uh-oh' in American English, you are using a glottal stop.

Five vowels (a,e,i,o,u) were used by the missionaries, but there are actually five more, the same vowels pronounced with a longer glide and more stress: ā, ē, ī, ō, and ū. A horizontal line (called a kahakō) is placed over these vowels. Nēnē, for example, is pronounced like "Nehh-Nehh" with a little 'a' in there, soft. We have attempted to include all kahakōs and 'okinas, so it will be easier for our readers to pronounce the words properly. Researching proper place names is a challenge, as some of the proper spellings and meanings are being lost. If we have made mistakes, we hope our more knowledgeable Hawai'ian readers will understand and let us know for future editions.

Each and every letter is pronounced in Hawai'ian, except for a few vowel combinations. However, locals often shorten names a bit, so listen carefully to the way natives pronounce a name.

Another addition to the language is a form of pidgin, which served to ease the difficulties of having multiple languages spoken. Laborers were brought in speaking Japanese, Mandarin, Cantonese, Portuguese, English, as well as other languages, and they had to be able to work together. Pidgin evolved as an improvised, but surprisingly effective way to communicate, and much of it survives in slang and common usage today. It's very interesting to hear and learn, but we'd suggest you be very circumspect about using it unless you study it carefully. It can sound affected from the mouth of a tourist, possibly coming off as if you're mimicing and disrespecting locals. It may be better to just listen and enjoy the lilt.

Pronunciation

Consonants are pronounced the same as in English, except that the
W sounds more like a V when it appears in the middle of a word.

Unstressed vowels are pronounced as follows:

a = *a* in *a*bove
e = *e* in b*e*t
i = *y* in cit*y*
o = *o* in s*o*le (without off glide)
u = *oo* in m*oo*n (without off glide)

Stressed vowels are a little different, and none have off glides:

a or ā = *a* in f*a*r
e = *e* in b*e*t
ē = between 'ehh' and *ay* in p*ay* *(not quite that hard)*
i or ī = *ee* in s*ee*
o or ō = *o* in s*o*le
u or ū = *oo* in m*oo*n

When pairs of vowels are joined (as they often are), pronounce each,
with slightly more emphasis on the first one. This varies somewhat
with local usage. It is beyond the scope of this book to teach the
complexities of spoken Hawaiʻian, but maybe we'll get you started.

Learning to respect and pronounce some Hawaiʻian will bring you
closer to the heart of the Hawaiʻian culture.Our goal is to make you
aware enough that you can understand what you are hearing, and not
be daunted by the many beautiful, but multisyllabic words.

Kealakekua, for example, is not so hard: it has four syllables: Ke.ala.
ke.kua and means: Ke (The) ala (pathway) (of) ke (the) kua (gods).
Now you're ready for humuhumunukunukuāpuaʻa (the state fish of
Hawaiʻi): humu.humu.nuku.nuku.āpu.aʻa. See, it's easy once you
divide it up!

After you get the hang of it, you may come to feel, as we have,
that Hawaiʻian is one of the most mellifluous languages on earth.
This may be part of the reasons songs in Hawaiʻian have become
popular far beyond the islands. Modern folksingers such as Iz (Israel
Kamakawiwaʻole) and Kealiʻi Reichel have contributed by writing
and singing beautiful new songs in Hawaiʻian. Listening to their new
as well as traditional songs is a great way to learn the pronunciation
of this delightful language!

Often Heard Myths

- *"You'll probably never see a shark."*

  If you snorkel often, you probably will see one occasionally, but a reef shark, not a great white or tiger shark. Reef sharks prefer seafood for dinner. If you look at actual statistics, your time is better spent worrying about lightning or pig attacks.

- *"Barracudas are harmless to humans."*

  Perhaps some are quite innocuous, but others have bitten off fingers or hands. The great barracuda has been involved in the majority of cases we've read. Don't worry about one that has been hanging out in front of a hotel for years, but you may not want to crowd them either. I'd be even more worried about eating one for dinner, because they are a definite, major cause of ciguatera "fish poisoning". They are one of the best tasting fish, though, in our experience. Feeling lucky?

- *"Jewelry attracts barracuda bites."*

  I first heard this rumor from a 12-year-old, and it was later reinforced by numerous books. The idea is that the flash will fool a barracuda into attacking. However, we've never verified a definite case of a person losing an ear lobe this way, even though I see people swimming and diving with earrings all the time. The same goes for wedding bands. I keep mine on and haven't had a problem.

- *"The water in Hawai'i is too cold for comfort."*
  "The water is Hawai'i is as warm as bath water."

  It can be pretty cool, especially late winter, especially if you go in naked (see *Basics*); but there is an alternative. Just wear a thin wetsuit and it will feel a lot like the Caribbean. Or you can wait till late summer and give the water a chance to warm up. Don't expect warm water particularly in Kaua'i, especially in the winter months.

- *"It rains all the time in Kaua'i."*
  "Kaua'i is too hot and sunny."
  "It's always windy in Kaua'i."

In Kaua'i you can have the climate of your choice. Don't believe everything you read in advertising literature (like hotel brochures) regarding perfect weather. It does vary, there are seasons, and location matters. It just depends on your personal preferences. You may hit a patch of rain, but it seldom lasts for long (though it can rain all week in the north at times!). The typical weather report for Po'ipū is Tonight — fair; Tomorrow, mostly sunny; for the weekend, sunny except for some upslope clouds in the afternoon. The drama of weather is part of the charm of the tropics — enjoy it as it is, rather than expecting it to be exactly as you want.

- *"Octopuses only come out at night."*

Some types are nocturnal, some not. We've seen lots in Hawai'i quite active during the day. The hard part is spotting them! Pay your dues, look sharp, and you'll see one eventually. The broad inner lagoon at 'Anini Beach is an excellent place to look.

- *"Kaua'i is getting too crowded and commercial."*

While there is certainly no problem buying a T-shirt in town or finding sun-worshippers on the beaches, there are plenty of spectacular sites to snorkel that are completely uncrowded. As long as you have a car, it's easy to drive to delightful and secluded locations — usually within half an hour from your hotel or condo. Hiking on Kaua'i can take you completely away from civilization as you know it, but a good map (such as ours) can lead you to some lovely snorkeling sites as well as romantic vistas to enjoy the sunset and the view of neighboring islands. And for really getting away from it all, try a snorkel trip to sunny Lehua Island.

Index

Achilles tang 142
Ahukini Landing 132
    map 133
'Aliomanu Beach 110
    map 111
Anahola State Park 114
    map 115
'Anini Beach 84
    map 85
authors 224

bannerfish 59
Barking Sands 181
    map 179
barracudas 30
basics 8
Beach House Beach 165
    map 163
bird wrasses 173, 207
Black Pot Beach 59
    map 57
blacktip reef shark 35, 209
body suit 14
bottlenose dolphin 210
Brennecke Beach 149
    map 151
butterflyfish 203

Cannons 47
caring for your gear 24
The Cliffs 74
cleaner wrasse 207
clearing your mask 22
cone shells 34
convict tang 18
cornetfish 202
crown of thorns sea star 69

damselfish 164
discounts 117

disposable underwater cameras
    90
dive boats 196
Doctor My Eyes 157
dolphins 209
Donkey Beach 118
    map 119
drowning 34

east area 96
    map 97
eels 33, 201
excursions 194
eyestripe surgeonfish 22, 109,
    207
feather duster worm 65, 105
filefish 206
fins 12
fourspot butterflyfish 204

gear selection 9
Gillin's Beach 147
    map 145
Glass Beach 172
    map 171
goldeye surgeonfish 108
great barracuda 30

Hā'ena Beach Park 48
    map 49
Hā'ena State Park 44
    map 45
Hanakā'ape Bay 161
    map 159
Hanakāpī'ai Beach 189
    map 185
Hanalei Pavilion Beach Park 58
    map 57
Hanamā'ulu Beach Park 130
    map 131

Hanapepe Beach Park 173
  map 171
Hāʻula Beach 143
  map 145
Hauwa 47
Hawaiʻian libraries 95
Hawaiʻian turkeyfish 33

hawkfish 112
hazards 26
Hideaways Beach 66
  map 67
Hōʻai Bay 162
  map 163
Holoholo Charters 194
humpback whale 211
Hurricane ʻIniki 87
hurricanes 87, 215
hypothermia 29

Infinities 177
ʻIniki, hurricane 87

Kalalau Beach 188
  map 185
Kalalau Trail 44, 188
Kalapakī Beach 136
  map 137
Kalihiwai Bay 88
  map 89
Kapaʻa Beach Park 122
  map 123
Kauaʻi Marriott 137
Kauaʻi road map 4
Kauaʻi Sea Tours 195
Kauapea Beach 92
  map 93
Kawailoa Beach 144
  map 145
Kaweonui Beach 75
  map 77
Kealia Beach 120
  map 123

Kēʻē Beach 44
  map 45
Kekaha Beach Park 180
  map 179
Keoneloa Beach 148
  map 141
Kepuhi Beach 52
  map 53
Kiahuna / Sheraton Beach 154
  map 155
Kīlauea Bay 99
Kīpū Kai 142
  map 145
Kōloa Landing 158
  map 159
Kukuiʻula Bay 168
Kumukumu Beach 118
  map 119

language 216
Larsen's Beach 104
  map 103
Lāwaʻi Bay 169
legend for maps 45
Lehua Island 190
  map 191
lei triggerfish 205
libraries 95
Līhuʻe area 130
  map 131
lobster 121
low volume masks 17
Lucy Wright Beach Park 177
Lumahaʻi Beach 54
  map 55
Lydgate Beach Park 126
  map 127

Māhāʻulepū beaches 145
Majors Beach 181
manta ray 200
manybar goatfish 177

marine life 198
mask 10
mask strap 12
milletseed butterflyfish 124
Miloli'i State Park 186
  map 187
Moloa'a Bay 106
  map 107
monk seal 166, 167
Moorish idol 11
motion sickness 21
movie locations 163
myths 218

Nā Pali Coast area 184
  map 185
Nāwiliwili Beach Park 136
  map 137
needlefish 202
Ni'ihau Island 190
  map 191
Ninini Beach 135
Niumalu Beach Park 139
northeast area 82
  map 83
northwest area 42
  map 43
Nu'alolo Kai State Park 186
  map 187
Nukoli'i Beach 128

octopus 180, 198
Often Heard Myths 218
orangeband surgeonfish 98

Pākalā Beach 177
Pali Ke Kua Beach 66
  map 67
Pāpa'a Bay 109
  map 103
parrotfish 157, 178, 205
peacock grouper 24

Picasso triggerfish 206
Pīla'a Beach 102
  map 103
Po'ipū area 140
  map 141
Po'ipū Beach 154
  map 155
Po'ipū Beach Park 150
  map 151
poisonous fish 33
Polihale State Park 182
  map 179
porcupinefish 208
Port Allen 171
Potter's angelfish 185
Prince Kūhiō Bay 162
  map 163
Princeville area 60
  map 61
Princeville Hotel 63
pufferfish 208
Pu'u Pōā Beach 62
  map 63
pyramid butterflyfish 130

Quarry Beach 99
Queen Emma's Bath 70
  map 71
Queen's Pond 182
  map 179

raccoon butterflyfish 129
rays 32, 200
rectangular triggerfish 71
reef shoes 14
reef squid 110, 165
reticulated butterflyfish 204
rip currents 28
rockmover wrasse 152, 153

saddleback butterflyfish 204

Salt Pond Beach Park 174
    map 175
scorpionfish 208
scrawled filefish 91, 206
Sea Fun Kaua'i 197
Sea Lodge Beach 75
    map 77
sea jellies 31
sea stars 200
sea turtles 173
sea urchins 30, 199
seasickness 21
Secret Beach 92
    map 93
sharks 35, 209
Sheraton / Kiahuna Beach 154
    map 155
Sheraton Princeville Hotel 62
Shipwreck Beach 148
shrimp 199
sign language 25
site index map 38
sites at a glance 40
snorkel 9
snorkel holder 9
snorkeling sites 36
snorkeling vest 16
Snuba® 81
southwest area 170
    map 171
spinner dolphins 209
spotted eagle ray 200
spotted pufferfish 193
spotted surgeonfish 206
spotted toby 87, 208
squirrelfish 139
sunburn 26
swim cap 16

teardrop butterflyfish 204
tides 214

tombolo 153
trevally jack 101
triggerfish 205
trumpetfish 145, 202
tsunamis 215
Tunnels 50
    map 49
turkeyfish 208
turtles 210

Wahiawa Bay 172
Wai'akalua Beach 100
    map 103
Waikoko Beach 56
    map 57
Wailua Beach 125
Wainiha Bay 52
    map 53
Wai'oli Beach Park 58
    map 57
Waipouli Beach Park 125
    map 123
water temperature 215
waves 27
weather 212
west area 178
    map 179
wetsuit 15
Whaler's Cove 161
    map 159
whales 211
Why Kaua'i? 6
wrasses 207
Wyllie's Beach 78
    map 79

yellowmargin surgeonfish 73
yellow tang 125
yellowtail coris 134, 135

About the Authors

Judy and Mel Malinowski love to snorkel in the warm oceans of the tropics.

This love has led them to embark on snorkeling and cultural adventures to 60-some countries from Anguilla to Zanzibar. Hawai'i kept drawing them back, infusing their lives with aloha and teaching respect of the 'aina.

Although they are certified Scuba divers, the lightness and freedom of snorkeling keeps it their favorite recreation. Whenever possible, they are in the water twice a day or more.

Mel, Judy and their three children have hosted students and cultural exchange visitors from Bosnia, Brazil, China, Germany, Nepal, New Zealand, Serbia, and Turkey in their home, and helped hundreds of other families enrich their lives through cultural exchange.

Working with exchange students and traveling as much as their businesses allow has encouraged their interest in the study of languages from Mandarin Chinese to Hawai'ian. They are graduates of Stanford University.

Mel and Judy live on the South Kohala coast of the island of Hawai'i.